AMERICAN BROTHER

ELISA M. CAMARA

HELLGATE PRESS   ASHLAND, OREGON

American Brother
©2013 Elisa M. Camara

Published by Hellgate Press

(An imprint of L&R Publishing, LLC)

Hellgate Press
PO Box 3531
Ashland, OR 97520
email: sales@hellgatepress.com

Editors: Michael Trudeau, Harley B. Patrick
Cover design: Douglas Nelson/*nelsoncreative.com*

For more about *American Brother:*
www.americanbrother.us • email*: elisa@americanbrother.us*
or visit American Brother on Facebook

Library of Congress Cataloging-in-Publication Data
Camara, Elisa.
American brother / Elisa Camara. -- First edition.
    pages cm
ISBN 978-1-55571-738-4
1. Camara, Mecot, 1960-1983. 2. Camara, Elisa--Family. 3. Brothers and sisters--West Virginia--Hinton--Biography. 4. United States Marine Compound Bombing, Beirut, Lebanon, 1983. 5. Marines--United States--Biography. 6. United States. Marine Corps--Biography. 7. Hinton (W. Va.)--Biography. 8. Cámara family. I. Title.
CT275.C265C35 2013
359.9'60973--dc23
[B]
                                    2013029924

Printed and bound in the United States of America
First edition 10 9 8 7 6 5 4 3 2 1

In honor of my only brother,
Sergeant Mecot E. Camara, United States Marine Corps.

With thanks to my three amazing sons, Joe, Sam, and Hank,
who inspire me daily, and especially to Cousin James,
who believed in me.

This book is written with love to Mecot Echo Camara, my brother's
only son and legacy to the Camara family in the United States.

Contents

Foreword

THE LAST TIME I STOOD BY SERGEANT MECOT E. CAMARA, he lay inside a silver transfer case, a kind of casket that the United States government uses to transport the bodies of her warriors killed in action. I remember looking at the two-inch wide strip of masking tape affixed to the foot of that casket and reading the one word written on it, "Camara." It matched the name on the roster that I had listing the Marines and other warriors among this shipment of those killed in the bombing in Beirut on October 23, 1983. My brothers, with whom I had served earlier in the year.

As the name, "Camara," registered in my mind, I gasped. A stab of pain struck my heart. I stood there looking down at the silver casket, and my emotions welled over my eyelids. I held my breath and gritted my jaws tight, but the tears that streamed off my cheeks gave away my particular grief. What a good Marine lay here! A damned fine Marine! I knew him well.

The name, "Camara," is one that sticks in the mind. But it was the smile of the man that wore the name that stuck more. A Marine filled with goodness, love of his family, his Marine Corps, and love of his country.

A sunny day in May, 1983; I will never forget it. When I think of Mecot Camara, his enthusiastic smile, I think of that day. He had become a fixture around the Marine Amphibious Unit headquarters element, and my crew. When I think of him, I see him that day. Wearing a t-shirt and his utility trousers, sweeping the asphalt parking lot where our General Purpose Medium tents stood, pegged into the pavement.

He never loafed. Not one to sit and watch clouds. So he grabbed a push-broom and went to work. A seemingly silly task. Sweeping up, around the tents. I stood at the sandbagged wall in front of the office door, coffee in my hand, and marveled at him. I laughed, and he beamed this great big smile at me.

There at the 24th Marine Amphibious Unit headquarters, inside the old firehouse and training facility—a long, concrete building with a few open bays and some offices—we could oversee the greater airport area. Across the way, a big, white warehouse of some sort stood with a big, white wall facing us. We used that white wall to project movies at night, when weather and relative safety allowed. Marines would sit on the pavement and watch some old flick. Corporal Camara (not yet Sergeant) made a point of sweeping the area where we sat.

My crew and I had absconded with an ugly black leather couch from the bombed-out United States Embassy weeks earlier. I usually sat on it, along with Gunnery Sergeant Steve Merrill and Staff Sergeant Jim Hickman. Sometimes Corporal Camara got to sit on it too. But most of the time he sat on the pavement with the rest of the junior ranks, so he kept the butt-hurting gravel swept off of it on movie night.

In those days, I was still new at being a Marine Warrant Officer. Gunner was the common term. I had graduated The Basic School at Quantico, Virginia on April 1, 1983, a class of April Fools. I caught a plane that very same day, bound to Beirut to relieve Captain Dale Dye as Deputy Public Affairs Officer for the Joint Public Affairs Bureau, Beirut.

Headquarters, U. S. Marine Corps had task organized the public affairs detachment, handpicked its members, and assigned us to Beirut, Lebanon in support of the Multinational Force, sent there to keep peace. We worked in essence as a support element for the commanding officer of the U. S. Forces assigned to the Multinational Force, but were directed by the Commandant of the Marine Corps. The official name did not include "Peacekeeping," although it was the mission and the media added it frequently.

I had known Captain Dye since he was a corporal and I was a private first class, Viet Nam the war ongoing then. And we were friends. I had last seen him seven months earlier in Denmark, September 1982. I had given him a ride in my rented BMW from Billund, in southern Jutland's rural Vejile County, to the northern tip of Denmark and our departure airport at Aalborg. We had been working NATO in northern Germany and across Denmark, especially busy in the central region around Karup and Viborg. The Commander Baltic Approaches was headquartered at Billund.

As those who also know Dale will attest, he can be rather demonstrative, especially when challenged. He is a Marine's Marine, after all. He swings through the trees with a knife in his teeth, among the best of us. An incident at the bar in Beirut's infamous Commodore Hotel had gotten him relieved of duties and sent packing home. One of the many international media who resided at the Commodore had commented to Dale about the latest "Rules of Engagement" made by the politicians in Washington, D.C. (people who knew nothing of war). Marines were not allowed to carry a loaded weapon. We could have loaded magazines, but we could not have them inserted in our rifles or pistols. The politicians had imagined that a Marine might accidently shoot someone if he carried a loaded firearm.

None of us liked that condition, plagued upon us mostly by micromanaging suits who had no clue, but we complied. When anyone might watch. On patrol, however, between you and me, I had my Marines locked and loaded. I'd rather face a court-martial than have dead Marines. I'd go to jail for my Marines. So would Dale Dye, and I know that Mecot Camara would too.

But we had to put on the good face for America and the world. Dale did that with aces. He told those reporters in the Commodore Hotel bar that it made no difference if the magazine was in or out of the weapon. A Marine could lock and load, and engage an enemy in a heartbeat anyway. And he demonstrated it with the forty-five he carried in his shoulder rig.

He locked, loaded, and then put the muzzle of his 1911A1 .45 ACP caliber pistol right in the face of the reporter who taunted him. One smooth heartbeat move. Oh, it was way too cool!

While several combat journalists found amusement in the antic, the man with the loaded and cocked gun up his nose found it quite disturbing. He complained. Cables transmitted to various news headquarters. Those noncombatant souls were even less amused. They complained.

A few weeks earlier, on February 2, 1983, a U.S. Marine captain named Charlie Johnson had mounted the nose of an Israeli Merkava (Hebrew for "Chariot") tank and challenged its commander and two other Merkava tanks near Checkpoint Charlie—a dingy little outpost over-watched by Lima Company, 3rd Battalion, 8th Marine Regiment, on the east side of the Beirut airport, overseeing the Sidon Road (site of many a firefight), an area we Marines fondly called, "Hooterville." Captain Charles B. Johnson stood against three Israeli tanks, armed only with a forty-five pistol. The trio of Israeli tanks retreated.

An American reporter happened to be there. Stories were told. The world press headlined the tale. Don Wright published a cartoon in The Miami News that took America by storm. An Israeli commander stands before the tank, addressing its crew: "You retreated? The Israeli Army never retreats! It was the odds, right? Syrian missiles, the Libyan Air Force and at least 50,000 armed-to-the-teeth Palestinians, right? How many? How many were you up against?" The tank commander, with head bowed, replies, "One U.S. Marine."

The world cheered the audacity of Captain Charlie Johnson.

What the story did not tell, nor did the reporter notice: several TOW missiles also pointed at the tanks. The incident gave Marines something grin about.

Dale had come close to getting almost the same level of press coverage, but negative. To placate the world media, Colonel James Meade, commanding officer of the soon-to-be-leaving 22nd MAU, sent Captain Dye home. It made the complaining press happy. Dale knew I was at

The Basic School, nearing graduation, so he recommended that I replace him. Good friend, Dale.

I arrived the day after my TBS graduation in sunny Beirut, Lebanon by way of a Pan American World Airways flight to London, then to Rome on another jet, then to Beirut aboard a Lebanese MEA Air-Liban jet. Pan-Am had suspended its flights to Beirut because of ground fire at the planes on landing and take-off. Air-Liban still flew, although the numbers of operating planes grew fewer and fewer as they crashed from the ground fire. Flying MEA was a thrill.

Dressed in a leather jacket, jeans, cowboy boots, and a Stetson hat, and fully strapped with a loaded U. S. Government Model, Series 70, Mark IV Colt .45 ACP pistol in a shoulder rig under my jacket, I stepped off the plane. My dear friend, Gunnery Sergeant Steve Merrill, greeted me. Steve and I had served in Japan together as staff sergeants. He had a good laugh at my looks. Yes, I replaced Big Daddy Dale Dye, but they still had the same brand of gun-slinging cowboy.

A tan-faced young Marine lance corporal stood by Gunny Merrill. His name was Steve Tingley. I remarked that I had a good friend who served with me in Okinawa in 1975 also named Steve Tingley. He was now a lieutenant in the Louisiana National Guard and lived in New Orleans. This kid, Tingley, did not have a clue nor any relation to the other Tingley.

Gunny Merrill called the lad, "Cadillac." So, from then on, I too called Tingley, "Lance Corporal Cadillac." It worked. Cadillac drove our truck and our jeep. He was one of the Marines assigned to the MAU S-3 by way of the Battalion Landing Team S-3. A gift to help us out.

On April 18, 1983, at approximately 1:00 p.m., a terrorist drove a truck bomb into the front of Post One at the United States Embassy, Beirut, which overlooked the Corniche, a seaside promenade along the Mediterranean. It was once upon a time, like much of Beirut had been years prior, a most beautiful drive. Lance Corporal Robert V. McMaugh, of Manassas, Virginia, an Embassy Marine from the Marine Security Guard Battalion, based at Quantico, VA, had stood at Post One. He took the brunt of the blast.

The barrel and receiver of his M16 rifle, that he had slung on his shoulder, wrapped itself around his back from the force of the explosion. The bowed rifle barrel still hangs on display along the memorial wall at Marine Security Guard Battalion headquarters. The bomb left a crater a dozen feet deep and thirty feet wide where the Embassy lobby had once stood at the center of the horseshoe shaped building.

Sixty-three people died in that bombing. Seventeen of the dead were Americans. One, a Marine, McMaugh. Several of the dead were Green Berets who died in the cafeteria, where I was supposed to be having lunch too. Except duty at the airport had delayed me.

A Marine standing watch along the airport perimeter had taken a bullet through his trouser leg, grazing his flesh. The media was hungry for a story. The Marine showed them the bullet hole in his trouser leg and the red mark on his leg. It was a big story at that moment.

Marines fired upon. But thirty seconds after the gaggle of press snapped pictures and asked for comments, the story fell to oblivion. Greater news had just taken place.

I recall hearing the blast. A sharp bang. Then I saw the plume of smoke. Major Jack Farmer, the 22nd MAU S-3 (operations officer) yelled at me to get a crew and "*di-di-mao*" (Vietnamese for run-run-immediately) to the American Embassy. Staff Sergeant Jim Hickman jumped in the back of my jeep and Sergeant Dave Luttenberger took the wheel. As we drove out, with a few extra arms packed with us, I told them to lock and load.

The press corps scrambled to their waiting Mercedes sedans, jammed in traffic far behind us. We left them in our dust. Luttenberger drove our jeep on sidewalks and through markets, getting past the jams.

We were the first Marines from the Multinational Force on the scene—the three of us. Chaos surrounded the American Embassy, razed to ruins, teargas filling the air, and we had to take charge of it. An hour or two later, a large force of armed Marines from the 22nd MAU, magazines in their rifles, arrived with Colonel "Large James" Meade at the lead. It was a Sunday when the bomb struck, and I did not lay down, much less even get a moment of sleep, until that Thursday night.

Until that Sunday, six months later, October 23, 1983, the U. S. Embassy bombing in Beirut, America's first terrorist attack, stood as the single deadliest attack against the United States since World War II. At least that's what the news reported. Peter Jennings came from London, along with the other first string press. The world watched Beirut.

April melded into May, and as the weather warmed to summer, likewise hostilities increased. At night, on the overlooking high grounds that rose on three sides of the airport, backgrounding our movies, we watched tracers arc across the hills, Katyusha rockets blasting neighborhoods and explosions sending fountains of fire into the air. We munched our MRE crackers and marveled.

Most of the fighting was between the Israeli-backed Phalangists (Lebanese Christian militia) and Lebanese Armed Forces, and the Syrian, Palestinian, and Iranian backed Muslim militias, the Druze and Amal, and the pro-Khomeini terrorists, Hezbollah.

Colonel Meade and his 22nd MAU packed their gear as the advanced party of the 24th MAU came ashore while the main body of their landing force arrived on station off the Lebanon shore. The Battalion Landing Team for the 22nd MAU was 1st Battalion, 8th Marine Regiment.

My old friend, from times as enlisted Marines with 3rd Reconnaissance Battalion, Captain Mike Haskell, was the S-3 Alpha–Assistant Operations Officer. He led the 24th MAU Advanced Party ashore weeks before the main body landed.

I chewed Red Man plug tobacco in those days. Nasty stuff. So strong it could eat through boiler plate steel. But it was a chew that many Marines preferred. Walking patrols in the heat, a plug of Red Man in the cheek kept a man mellow. Happy, in fact.

It was part of my breakfast. A cup of coffee and a plug of Red Man in my cheek made life good. It also flavored my beer, when I could get some beer. Young Marines marveled at the "Gunner," as they called me, because I could drink anything with Red Man in my cheek, and never even get dizzy. It was grizzly and impressed the young Marines to no end. A John Wayne brand of Spartan leadership.

Corporal Camara and many others of our salty young crew also chewed. Most of them preferred Beechnut.

Major Christian Metz, the Commanding Officer of the French Marine Corps' 9th Demi (short term for demi-brigade), a friend I made in Beirut, and who later came to Quantico where he studied at the U. S. Marine Corps Command and Staff College and lived in base housing near me, tried chewing some of my Red Man one morning in Beirut. Corporal Camara was there with a few other admiring troops.

I had told Major Metz that chewing tobacco was what many of us called, "cowboy candy." Very good stuff. Quite pleasant. Tobacco also in their cheeks, Camara and my boys agreed and offered their enthusiasm at the French Marine trying a chew.

"Go ahead, sir," I can still hear Corporal Camara urging the Frenchman.

I cut off a square of Red Man from my plug, and gave it to Major Metz. He tucked it in his cheek. I warned him not to swallow. However, I don't think he could help but swallow, because he could not stop spitting from the profusion of saliva that his mouth immediately generated.

He began getting dizzy, turned pale green and then violent nausea set in. After enduring great pain, fighting the good fight, Major Metz heaved out the chew with a big blow of spit.

Corporal Camara and the gang erupted, laughing.

"Zis is ze most horrible experience of my life!" Metz gasped.

Even more laughter.

Bad thing about chewing Red Man, when a man runs out of it, he becomes cranky. When a Marine Gunner runs out of his chew, he will bite off the heads of baby kittens. Or it seems that way to the enlisted troops surrounding him. I thought that I maintained myself rather well, but they didn't. They avoided me like a bad smell.

With the transition from the 22nd MAU to the 24th MAU, the so-called PX closed down. No more Red Man or Beechnut until the 24th MAU re-opened the store around the first week of June.

One day, Major Fred Lash, my boss, the Public Affairs Officer for the Joint Public Affairs Bureau, handed me a box with "Gunner Henderson" written on the brown cardboard. I opened it and inside was a case of Beechnut Chewing Tobacco. A dozen or more red-and-white stripped pouches of wonderful, sweet chew.

"Iron Mike sent that ashore for you," Fred said. Major Lash had known Sergeant Mike Haskell at 3rd Recon too. Apparently, on his sojourns out to the approaching ships, Captain Haskell had found a store of chewing tobacco, and sent a box ashore to me on one of the MarLog mail and logistics helicopter flights.

So, as I stepped out of the MAU headquarters on this bright and sunny day in May, a wonderful chew of Beechnut in my cheek and a cup of hot coffee hanging on my finger, I leaned my elbow on the stack of sandbags and looked out at my happy world. Gunny Merrill stood at my side. Corporal Cadillac sat, eating an MRE, on one of the dirty red airline seats that we had salvaged from a crashed MEA-Air Liban jetliner set inside our General Purpose Medium tent with the sides rolled up—our sleeping quarters. Cadillac had extended his tour in Beirut.

In the parking lot, Corporal Camara swept away dirt and pebbles with his push broom, a big wad of Beechnut in his cheek. I had taken two pouches for myself, and distributed the rest among our Marines, including a pouch for Corporal Camara. I think that Captain Haskell knew I would share the wealth that way.

By the end of May, Mike Haskell and company had set up his S-3 shop down the hill in the big, four-story building that we had named, "The Beirut Hilton." Colonel Tim Geraghty moved into the office and quarters above our shop, commanding the 24th MAU, and Lieutenant Colonel Howard Gerlach, commanding officer of the 1st Battalion, 8th Marine Regiment's Battalion Landing Team opened his command post with Haskell and the bulk of his battalion.

Colonel Geraghty did not like the wide disbursement of the Marine units, so he began consolidating them for greater firepower and protection, and building bunkers. As the Marines bunkered up, the hostile forces turned their guns more-so toward the peacekeepers.

A week or two before Colonel Meade and the 22nd MAU had departed our company, he had obtained a young, black billy goat for a barbecue. Problem with Marines and baby goats, just like puppies, they become pets not food. In a matter of days, the barbecue meal had switched from roasted goat to hamburgers. Now, the little black goat with sprouting horns became a fixture around the MAU headquarters, dropping his goat pills where he liked, and nibbling on anything that a Marine might give him.

Major Fred Lash named him "General Billy." And all the Marines enjoyed having General Billy among us. Everyone except the MAU Sergeant Major. General Billy used to crap on the sergeant major's cot, and right next to it. It was almost as if General Billy knew what he was doing. Knew that the sergeant major hated him and wanted him dead. So General Billy copped an attitude with the sergeant major.

Gunner Frankie Fields from Radio Battalion kept watch over the goat, giving him a baby bottle of milk several times a day. He taught Corporal Camara to bottle feed General Billy too. It was quite entertaining to watch General Billy come running for his bottle. Captain Haskell also assigned Corporal Camara the duties of keeping General Billy out of trouble, and away from the sergeant major's rack.

I laughed on many a morning, seeing Corporal Camara spiriting away General Billy, after he had visited the sergeant major's tent, cleaning up the droppings before the sergeant major could find the mess on his cot and next to it.

The goat lived on borrowed time. Literally.

While a joke among many, the commanding officer did not need the distraction. He gave us marching orders to find a solution to the goat problem. Yes, the pet, our unofficial mascot, had become a command problem.

Out of necessity, trying to keep General Billy alive, I dreamed up the idea of contacting the City of Pasadena, California and the Rose Bowl Committee. The city fathers there had wanted to do something at that year's Rose Bowl that would recognize the Marines in Beirut. I suggested that since the United States Navy had a white goat as its mascot at Annapolis, that Marines should correspond with a black goat from Beirut. The Pasadena folks liked the idea and we set the wheels turning.

Corporal Camara and General Billy had a mission: The Rose Bowl.

After I had departed Beirut in the summer of 1983, Corporal Camara and his cohorts delivered General Billy to an awaiting Pan-American World Airways flight to the United States via Rome. Before I had left, I had coordinated with people at the United States Embassy to get General Billy the necessary health papers and vaccinations to allow him entry into the United States. It took awhile, but Corporal Camara and the other Marines who protected the black billy goat got it done.

General Billy had made it through the plane change at Rome without a problem. However, when he landed at Kennedy International Airport in New York his luck ran out. Despite having all the documentation, vaccination, and quarantines in order, the knuckleheads working at United States Customs at Kennedy Airport did not bother to look at any documents. All they saw was a black billy goat in a box. It was alive! It needed to be dead!

They euthanized General Billy on the spot. No explanation.

Of course, the City of Pasadena, California and the Rose Bowl Committee were gravely upset, as were we Marines who had regarded General Billy as our mascot and friend. And perhaps even the MAU sergeant major also shared in that final regret.

I have a photograph on the back of the first edition hardcover of my book, *Marine Sniper*, showing me eating a C-ration lunch outside my tent in Beirut, and General Billy standing there, begging for a bite.

Corporal Camara was there that day too. My friend Claude Salhani, then a reporter and photographer for United Press International, took the picture.

I cannot look at that picture, and the goat, without also remembering Sergeant Mecot E. Camara. In fact, I cannot think of my life in Beirut without thoughts of then Corporal Camara entering my mind. The big smile, the push broom, and the black billy goat that he lead by a piece of rope. General Billy chasing after Corporal Camara and his baby bottle of milk.

Camara and Cadillac and Iron Mike Haskell, and so many others of my brothers that we lost that hurtful day—October 23, 1983. They remain with me.

When Elisa Camara contacted me, wanting to use a quote from something that I had written about Beirut and Captain Mike Haskell, whose family remain in contact with me today, she had no idea that I knew her big brother. She only knew that her brother had thought the world of Captain Haskell, his officer-in-charge. We connected, and I also put her in touch with Captain Haskell's widow, Christine, and two children, now grown, Melissa and Jason.

I could not help but shed tears and choke up as I told her so many stories of her brother and the others in Beirut. And how I had spent those many sleepless days and nights at Dover Air Force Base, bringing them home: Overseeing the unloading of the planes, the Marine volunteers handling each casket, carrying them one at a time with solemn honor and greatest respect. Ensuring that the caskets were arranged exactly right in the big C-5 hangar where we held memorial services each morning with every arrival of our dead. Speaking to the bereaved family members who came to Dover Air Force Base for their sons and brothers and husbands and fathers. I told Elisa of the emotional battle I fought with myself, showing these family members a strong, caring Marine on the outside, while sobbing for their losses on the inside.

A day after the bombing, I had packed a bag and all of my class-A uniforms, and drove from Quantico to Dover. Since I had served with the 24th Marine Amphibious Unit, the Commandant of the Marine Corps regarded it only appropriate that I should serve as a Marine liaison and press officer to bring our warriors home. Had he not chosen me, I would have requested mast, demanding that I go. I certainly could not stay home.

To this day, regardless of clime or threat, my two weeks at Dover, bringing home our warriors who fell in Beirut on October 23, 1983, remains the toughest duty, and most memorable, I have ever stood.

Each day as I walked along the lines of caskets, reading the names off my roster, and matching those names with those written on the masking tape affixed to the foot of each silver case that contained one of my brothers, my heart broke and broke again.

The day I saw Elisa's brother's name, along with Haskell and Tingley, was the toughest day of all.

We must never forget our sons and daughters who give up their lives and their limbs, and the very best parts of their inner beings, to the People of the United States of America. They did not die for any government or political purpose, but for the sake of freedom and decency among humanity.

I am eternally grateful that Elisa chose to write her book about her big brother—her American Brother. This way, America can know him as a person. A brother who loved his sister, his mother, his wife, and his own son. This way, people can know his greatness and his goodness.

I know without question that Mecot E. Camara and all his brothers who fell with him that day in Beirut were there for the purpose of carrying out God's love to mankind, and not war. They sought peace!

It was about the children. It was about the struggling families. It was about the mother I saw on patrol along the Green Line in Beirut one day, getting water from a broken pipe, cooking on an open fire, and living with her small, frail, and frightened little girl beneath a great slab of broken concrete. These punished poor, who had done nothing wrong but live between warring factions, needed our help. Mecot Camara and America's Marines came to help.

We died and we bled for them.

—Charles W. Henderson, Chief Warrant Officer,
United States Marine Corps, Retired

1

Creation of an American Brother

A S THE VIBRANT COLORS OF GOLD, ORANGE, AND YELLOW slowly began to shimmer down the Appalachian mountainside, the end of October was nearing. November would bring barren trees, chilled air, and the smell of warm fireplaces cranking up for the first time. Yummy Thanksgiving turkey and homemade pumpkin pie baking in Mom's oven could not have motivated me more to get back home from college.

My family had been completely engaged in preparations for a special Thanksgiving celebration in honor of my twenty-two-year-old brother, Sergeant Mecot E. Camara, who was returning from Beirut, Lebanon. He had received his military orders from the Twenty-Fourth Marine Amphibious Unit of the United States Marines on March 24, 1983, to serve as part of an international peacekeeping mission in Beirut. It was now eight months later, and he had a whole family waiting for him: mom, little sister, big sister and brother-in-law, two aunts and their families, a wife, and a nineteen-month-old son—not to mention the entire population of Hinton, West Virginia, where he grew up. We were all so proud of him.

It all began with our parents. They met at Mount Sinai Hospital in Miami, Florida, in 1956. Mom was an all-American blond, blue-eyed nurse named Billie Jean Hoskins from Lexington, Kentucky, and Dad was a handsome Filipino doctor finishing his residency in general surgery. His name was Prudencio Beduya Camara. He entered the United States through Anchorage, Alaska, in 1955. They were married in 1957 and lived in Miami for two years. That's where my older sister, Threase, was born in December of 1958.

Later they moved to Nashville, Tennessee, where Daddy was going to complete his residency. This is also where my big brother was born on December 28, 1960. He was given the first name Ramon after our dad's brother and the middle name Eugene after my mother's uncle. He may have been named Ramon, but that name didn't last long. Within a few short months, his birth name was replaced with the nickname "Mecot." And how did that happen...?

My brother was born with a large mole on the left side of his head. Daddy had it removed while he was still a baby. However, the surgery left him with a speech defect. Of course my parents were quick to respond, being in the medical field, and they had him undergo extensive speech therapy.

In the meantime, Threase was my brother's voice until he learned to speak. During his toddler years, he and Threase would often play with their imaginary friend "Mrs. Goodwitch." And on one snowy afternoon, Mrs. Goodwitch remamed Ramon to "Mecot" while sharing a fabulous tea party for three! Subsequently, I discovered that our Aunt Gemma indicated that in the Philippines, *mecot* is a term of endearment. Threase must have learned this from our aunt at a younger age. So until Mecot began verbalizing on his own, Threase, with the help of Mrs. Goodwitch, would tell Mom and Dad almost everything he wanted or needed.

My family will tell you that not only was Mecot born with a large mole on his face but that he also had a more noticeable, and infamous, smirky grin! His smirky grin could get him out of any trouble he ever got himself into. Eventually, he did begin speaking, and when asked his name, with his smirky little grin he always responded "Mecot." So the name Mecot stuck with him for the rest of his life.

Mom and Dad's wedding in Miami Beach, Florida, on April 26, 1958.

Our dad stayed in Nashville and completed three more years of surgical training in Saint Thomas Hospital and one full year there as chief resident. After his training, he worked for one year with Dr. Sidney Waynewright Ballard in downtown Nashville. Daddy then had three medical opportunities to choose from: 1) Charlotte, North Carolina; 2) Shreveport, Louisiana; or 3) Hinton, West Virginia.

Hinton was an option because he had met a college friend of his in Richmond, Virginia, who told him he was going to Point Pleasant, West Virginia, and that Hinton, a quaint little town, was on the way. His friend said he could ride with him and catch up on the last ten years since that had graduated together.

Daddy was so glad he went on that little road trip because it was then he fell in love with Hinton. His friend's little VW bug winded around the curvy roads beside the rolling rivers and they could hear the sounds of the railroad trains chugging along the side of the mountains. Downtown Hinton was lined with deep red brick streets, and it was centered right in the heart of the valley. This little town was nestled among the rivers and mountains. Even more appealing than the scenery was the kindness of Hinton's townsfolk. He really fell in love with the people of Hinton.

Daddy and his friend stopped for ice cream at the local diner. He was in awe at the kind people in the café that day. The laughs and smiles were contagious. There was everything from railroad workers off the clock to coal miners fresh from the mines enjoying one another's company while eating a warm meal of baked chicken, peas, and rolls.

Most of the railroaders wore dirty overalls from shoveling coal into the train furnaces. And the coal miners were covered in coal dust and soot. Their hands were wrinkled and hardened and appeared permanently stained a deep black. But the café owner didn't mind one bit. They seemed to all know each other. And despite their untidiness, the owner greeted them with a warm smile and a cool beverage of their choice.

These gentlemen noticed Daddy and his friend. It was a very small town where everyone knew one another. They did not know Daddy and were not shy to meet him. After the firm handshakes and introductions, Daddy told them he was driving through town looking for somewhere to open his medical practice. When they found out Daddy was a doctor they were so excited! The local hospital was in need of another doctor. And they were smitten by Daddy's warmheartedness and contagious smile. He felt the same for them.

Daddy being welcomed to Hinton Hospital by Dr. W.J. VanSant (*left*) as
Minnie Fitzsimmons and Elizabeth Mann look on, ca.1965.

He later applied for that position at Hinton Hospital and was offered
the job, which he graciously accepted. While he started his new medical
practice, my mother became pregnant with me. A surprise from the
good Lord, I suppose! So I came along in October 1965. I was born in
Bluefield, West Virginia, just up the mountain in the neighboring city.

My father worked in the Hinton Hospital for two years, during which
time the townsfolk of Hinton really got to know him. They just adored him.
They could sense his warm heart and genuine concern for their health.
Every day he would come home with homemade jams, jellies, beautiful
knitted blankets, and fresh vegetables from his patient's gardens. Soon after becoming the town doctor of Hinton, he received his U.S. citizenship
and passed the state boards. He opened his own private practice and began
surgical operations at the newly opened Summers County Hospital.

It was a big day when he received his U.S. citizenship. I was only a toddler at the time, but my mother told me stories of the lavish celebration the community of Hinton had for him and our family. Mecot and my sister skipped around in celebration, waving the little American flags that they'd pulled from the centerpieces in the banquet room.

Mecot witnessed at a young age how much our family and our town exuded a fond affection for our country and how it valued our citizenship. Not to mention the devotion my dad had for his freedoms here and his ability to help people by building his medical practice in Hinton.

So my family officially settled into Hinton, West Virginia. After renting for a few months, my dad bought the house of Mr. and Mrs. Garnet Willey at 1008 Greenbrier Drive. When Daddy bought the house, the yard was quite big. He looked around and told himself there were many possibilities, and a few years later he landscaped the yard.

An article appeared in the *Charleston Gazette* described Daddy's handiwork:

> For three years he designed plans for a garden with an Oriental and Occidental flavor. After two years of building he succeeded.
>
> The entrance to his garden, a showplace in Summers County, contains a 4-foot statue of the Madonna carved out of marble and shipped to Hinton from Rome.
>
> The work wasn't easy. Doctor Camara first had to cut away a sloping hillside to install an underground pumping system for a fountain. Then he had to construct retaining walls to prevent possible landslides.
>
> The walkway is lined with rhododendrons and more than 50 different plants.
>
> The fountain and pond are filled with goldfish and a carp from Japan [that] lives for 100 years. Glass in the fountain is hand-carved.
>
> The garden is wired for music and is equipped with underground lighting and speaker systems. A plaza, set with inlaid

pieces of colored slate from Colorado, is surrounded by beds of petunias and roses.

An oak handbridge connects the garden's entry to the plaza. A pine tree, with limbs spreading in an Oriental look, provides shade for the garden.

When the garden was completed in 1970, Doctor Camara installed a sign above the pond which reads: "The kiss of the sun for pardon, the song of the earth for mirth, you're closer to God in a garden than anywhere else on earth."[1]

My dad's medical office was doing very well in town, and my mother was working alongside him as a nurse. However, when he opened his office, he thought the whole venture was rather daring, because there had been some insinuation that he would not be successful.

There were other foreign doctors ahead of him who had tried to open an office, but they had left town due to lack of business. But his practice turned out very successful, and when the Summers County Hospital opened he started his surgical practice there too.

During the day, Threase, Mecot, and I stayed at home with an amazing babysitter. She was a kindhearted older woman who was born and raised in Hinton. We called her "Nanny." She pretty much raised my sister and brother and me, since my mom was at the medical office with my dad much of the time.

She taught me all about canning vegetables and baking yummy cakes and pies. And she could string beans faster than anyone ever could. We would sit outside on her front-porch rocking bench with a bushel of green beans and a paper bag. She would rock that porch bench, sing gospel, and string beans like nothing I had ever seen before.

Nanny grew up in the mountains. She was a very Christian lady; moreover, she was quite the disciplinarian. One time Mecot came home with muddy, muddy shoes after he had been playing along the riverbank trying

---

1 Terry Wimmer, "Garden Taste of Home," *Charleston Gazette*, August 30, 1976.

Fun family times celebrating my birthday with Threase (*left*)
and Mecot, 1969.

to catch crawdaddies. Mecot caught a few, alright. He came running in the
front screen door with a bucketful, tracking mud through the house. He
even managed to drop a few of those creepy-crawlies along the way.

The splish-splosh of his sopping socks and old canvas tennis shoes
preceded his screams of excitement. It still amazes me that catching a
bucketful of crawdaddies could be so exciting! What was even more exciting was witnessing Nanny exploding because of the trail of dark
brown mud tracks Mecot left all around the house. That was more than
enough to get Nanny going!

My dad had planted an apple orchard in the front yard that yielded the
most delicious apples you could ever bite into. They were tart, juicy green

apples. But Nanny had another use from that orchard other than picking and eating those apples. Although she made some yummy applesauce with those apples, those branches made the best "switches" ever.

Needless to say, my brother knew what was coming. Rarely did Nanny have to resort to the switch, but when she did you just knew you were in big trouble—but not for Mecot.

For some reason, Mecot always declared he never really got into trouble. It's just that trouble always found him, and usually his smirky grin was all he needed to get himself out of it. He had his own little charm that always worked in his favor. As a result, Nanny's switches never made contact with Mecot's brown little behind. Now, my behind is a whole other story.

But in addition to our Nanny taking care of us during the day, we also had living with us for a few years our two aunts direct from the Philippines. They came to America in the late sixties and made Hinton their home too! Daddy wanted to send over two of his eighteen siblings to help them complete their education.

Aunt Era and Aunt Gemma moved into our basement for a short while. They brought with them a sense of jubilance and infectious high energy that lingered throughout our home until they moved into a downtown apartment in Hinton a few years later.

While they resided at our home, Mecot would constantly be right in the midst of their high energy. My aunts were musically talented. They could sing and dance, play the guitar and piano like nothing you have ever heard or seen before in America. They sang with a passion that exuded from every melodic word they would vocalize. And their dances were a combined seventies disco with a little bit of two-steppin' thrown in.

Mecot, just like his Filipino aunts, was far from shy. And although at times we couldn't understand our aunts' broken English, Mecot had a way of figuring them out. On cool summer evenings, gathered around our front porch, I would be endlessly trying to catch fireflies while hearing their singing and dancing echoing off the mountainside. And yes, Mecot could

Aunt Era, Daddy and Aunt Gemma full of
cheer ready to greet guests for our annual
Christmas Party, 1973.

be seen wiggling his hips and tapping his toes while the sound of his voice
could be heard from the mountaintops, blending right in with the whimsi-
cal music of our aunts. They would teach him Filipino songs and he'd
teach them top '70's American band songs like "Freebird" by Lynyrd
Skynyrd, "American Pie" by Don McLean, and "Play That Funky Music"
by Wild Cherry. Our Filipino aunts always said we were a family that was
loud, that laughed a lot, and that loved much!

Mecot possessed the loud, the laughter and the love qualities for sure!
His smirky grin was infectious and his belting out songs with our aunts
was a testimony to his love of life.

It's hard to believe those childhood years went by so fast. Now it was 1983 and we were preparing the best Thanksgiving ever. My aunts prepared the traditional Filipino feast comprised of siopao, pancit, and chicken adobo. Siopao means steamed buns filled with different varieties of meats like chicken or beef. Pancit means noodles and fresh vegetables (celery, carrots, onions, and the like) that are usually cooked together. Lastly, chicken adobe (the national food of the Philippines) is the cooking process in Philippine cuisine that involves meat or seafood marinated in a sauce of vinegar and garlic, sautéed in oil, and simmered in the marinade. Yes, we had chicken adobe served at our Thanksgiving dinner, as well as turkey and the best fried rice in all of the good ole United States.

It was the fall of 1983, and Mecot would be coming home for Thanksgiving soon.

2

Beirut Bound

I SUPPOSE LIVING A SIMPLE LIFE IN a small town somewhat sheltered me from global happenings. Obviously, there was a lot transpiring in the world around 1982—most especially in Beirut, Lebanon, where turmoil was running rampant and peace seemed impossible. However, help was on its way for this war-torn nation, as other countries decided to join together and send their own militaries, right along with ours, to act as peacekeepers.

According to several Internet sources, there was a clear plan in place:

> ...the Beirut mission started out as an effort to stabilize a fragile peace in a war-torn country. Lebanon had been in turmoil since the Palestine Liberation Organization, having been expelled from Jordan, took refuge there in the 1970s. In 1975, groups of Christian and Muslim militias, some backed by neighboring powers such as Iran, Syria, and Israel, turned what had been a Middle East oasis into a no-man's-land of urban warfare.
>
> Israel invaded in 1982, hoping to crush the PLO. In exchange for an Israeli withdrawal, the United Nations sent in a peacekeeping force made up of troops from Great Britain, France, Italy, and the United States.

I graduated from Hinton High School in May of 1983. Mecot had been sending me letters frequently, advising me on colleges that he would like to see me attend. He was determined that I start and finish at a good college no matter what! He was shocked that I wanted to attend an all-female college by the name of Queens College in Charlotte, North Carolina. He would write, "I know you well. There must be an all-boys school close by. I can't imagine you at school four years with no football players close by to date. You know, Daddy always suggested you join the convent—ha!"

However, on my graduation day as I was heading down the aisle with all the pomp and circumstance, I felt Mecot was there guiding and supporting me all the way down to the auditorium stage straight to my diploma. I sensed Mecot shouting in my ear, "Go sis, go!"

Little did I know I really should have been cheering on Mecot. He had a big assignment ahead of him. It was probably bigger than he and most Americans (including myself) could imagine. The Twenty-Fourth Marine Amphibious Unit embarked on May 11, 1983, for its peacekeeping mission on Middle Eastern shores. They left base at Camp Lejeune, North Carolina, and boarded ship at Port of Morehead City, North Carolina.

Mecot told me it was a long journey aboard ship, but there were times that allowed the guys to blow off steam. One event Mecot participated in was the "Steel Beach Picnic." While on the landing platform Mecot and a few of his comrades had the privilege of squirting a fire hose at a basketball, trying to get it into a bucket that sat on deck. He lived by the motto "Work hard, play hard."

After weeks on the ship, the two thousand Marines of the Twenty-Fourth MAU finally landed to relieve a grateful Twenty-Second MAU in late May. Their mission was to work with British, French, and Italian peacekeepers to calm elements of the violent Lebanese civil war, keep the Beirut International Airport open, and provide a presence so that no fighting erupted.

Mecot (*right*) and fellow Marines (Thomas Stowe and Timothy McNelly) in a competition named "Steel Beach Picnic" aboard ship en route to Beirut. They won the competition which involved trying to get a basketball into a bucket on the flightdeck of the ship by squirting it with a firehose. (Photo courtesy of Dan Joy)

Initially, the U.S. forces, along with the French and Italian forces, provided a measure of stability. However, as diplomatic efforts failed to achieve a basis for a lasting settlement, the differing factions came to perceive the Marines as enemies. This led to artillery, mortar, and small-arms fire directed at the Marine Corps positions daily.

While Mecot was serving as peacekeeper and trying to stay clear of enemy fire in Beirut, I was beginning my freshman year at Queens College in Charlotte.

Mecot would write letters reporting the enemy activity from the hills. His troops referred to the battalion landing team (BLT) building as the "Beirut Hilton," and they felt safe and protected there. But unfortunately, it did make for an easy target for enemy warfare. The enemy was surrounding them from the tops of the hills while Mecot and the Marines sat at the bottom of the hills, in a valley.

The marine compound was often attacked by various methods, such as rifle fire, grenade, booby trap, or car bomb. Precautions were taken to guard against such dangers, but life within the Marine compound varied little from any normal deployment. The Marines conducted their training, found time for jogging and other physical fitness, worked on Marine Corps Institute correspondence courses, and broke the monotony by reading, playing cards, joking around with their fellow Marines, and writing letters home.

Mecot would send letters home asking for us to send candy and balloons for the Lebanese children. He told us they would walk by the headquarters and look at him through the barbed-wire fencing. He knew they had a high sense of curiosity and he felt bad for them living in such daily turmoil.

He remembered how fortunate we were growing up in our small town. Our home sat nestled between the river and the mountainside much like Beirut; but it was free from war and grief. We were blessed with Mother Nature's peaceful playground of rivers to fish and swim in as well as mountains for hiking and biking. We had an abundance of play toys, from buckets of army soldiers to Easy-Bake Ovens. And Mecot wanted these kids to have a little bit of happiness that we were fortunate to have growing up.

Once he received the candy and balloons from us, he would pass them through the fencing for the kids. He would tell us they were smiling and giggling while expressing their sheer happiness to receive these things. They would leave with big smiles on their faces, saying in broken English, "Thank you, U.S. Marine. Thank you." So Mecot got in the habit of requesting candy and balloons in each letter.

And of course, I can't forget his ongoing request for Beech-Nut chewing tobacco! It never took much to make Mecot happy, and that even goes for being shipped to Beirut without the luxuries of everyday life at home. However, Mecot loved his chewing tobacco. He chewed Beech-Nut, and only Beech-Nut, and he was very happy knowing that it was something that could be sent to him from home. He chewed regularly when he was not chowing down on food or drinks. You always knew when he had some in his mouth because one cheek was always three times the size of the other. But somehow he would still manage to pull off the smirky grin with a cheekful of Beech-Nut.

Little did he complain about, although he would write that he wasn't crazy about shaving from a cold pan of water, jerry-rigging the lights and the radio to get them to work, and washing his clothes in a tiny sink. He also shared that he had clothes strung all over his room. I am sure he was missing the things we so often took for granted at home, like bathroom sinks and a washer and dryer.

As the months passed, I could sense in his letters that things were turning turbulent in Beirut. He took his role as sergeant very seriously. Although he would always make clear in his letters that he was with the finest elite troops in the world, he would write about his concerns for his troops' safety around the BLT headquarters. He did write in one of his letters that he had to go because of an alert drill and it was his time to do his part for the boys.

3

Blast Hits Queens College

I T WAS A COOL, CRISP FALL DAY AT Queens College, Charlotte, North Carolina. The leaves on the enormous oak trees were just beginning to project vibrant hues of orange and yellow. I was a small-town seventeen-year-old freshman from West Virginia ready to engage in an exciting college career.

Queens was perfect for me. It was an all-female college tucked away just outside downtown Charlotte amid beautiful antebellum homes. And the southern hospitality was very warm and inviting among the students, faculty, and surrounding neighborhood.

I was getting settled into my new life away from home and learning the new routine of early-morning classes and late-night partying and gaining the "freshman fifteen" from starchy cafeteria food.

I lived in Belk Dorm with my roommate from my small town in West Virginia. Her name was Becky, and our families were very fond of each other. My dad was their family doctor and we had become acquainted in high school.

Belk Dorm housed only the freshman class and it was there I learned all about communal living. Our dorm rooms were not wired for cable TV, so we gathered in the afternoons in the lobby to watch our favorite soap operas and in the evenings to watch our favorite sitcoms.

On October 23, 1983, I recall walking back to Belk Dorm from my 8:00 a.m. English class. As I walked by the lobby, I noticed a small gathering of fellow freshmen already watching TV. This was a little odd to me, considering it was early in the morning.

The great thing with media is that when news happens it is broadcast almost immediately, even back in the eighties. Little did I know that my friends' eyes were all fixed on the news that morning. Unaware of the unfolding tragedy, I walked down my hallway in a complete fog and into my dorm room. My life was about to change forever.

As I unlocked the door to my secure haven, complete with wall flowers decals, an Oriental rug, and Smurf decorations everywhere (I was totally into the Smurfs—yes, at seventeen years old—whose happy, perky, and constantly smiling images of cheerful bliss were contagious), I suddenly felt my warm, happy home turn into a cold, four-walled room of complete shock and terror.

My dad had given me a tiny Sony Trinitron TV when I turned sixteen years old, and I'd brought it to college. No one had a portable Sony Trinitron back then. (He won it at a physicians' conference.) Though our dorm rooms did not have cable hookups in 1983, we did get limited reception from the local TV networks. That morning, while I was at my 8:00 a.m. class, Becky had turned on the TV to discover the disturbing news that a bomb had exploded at the Marine compound in Beirut, and that there were fatalities. When I entered our room, she looked at me with disbelief and fear in her eyes. She told me what she had been watching on the TV, which is exactly what I had just walked by in the Belk Dorm lobby.

After trying relentlessly to get good reception and being unable to do so, I realized that I could run to the lobby and watch it with better reception on that TV. By this time more of my friends were there watching. I was shocked to see so many awake already, standing motionless with eyes fixated on the screen. The lobby was twice as full as it was ten minutes earlier when I walked by the first time.

At 6:22 a.m. October 23, 1983, a large yellow Mercedes Benz delivery truck drove to the airport, turned onto an access road leading to the BLT 1-8 building [known as "the

October 23, 1983, 6:20 a.m. A smoke cloud rises from the rubble of the bombed barracks at Beirut International Airport.

barracks" or the "Beirut Hilton" to most of the Marines], sped up, circled the parking lot once, and drove through the barbed-wire fence, passed between two sentry posts, received no fire, slammed through the gate, passed around one sewer-pipe barrier and between two others, ploughed through the sergeant-at-arms sandbag fortification, and crashed into the lobby of the barracks and detonated. It is estimated that the force of the explosion was equal to more than 12,000 lbs. of TNT, bringing much of the building to the ground instantly. Colonel Geraghty said the device had 21,000 lbs. of explosives. Staff Sergeant Randy Gaddo has said the truck had 2,000 pounds of dynamite strapped around gas cylinders,

which [together] was the equivalent of 20,000 lbs. of TNT.
There was a fireball which ripped through the concrete. The
FBI reported that it was the largest non-nuclear bomb in history. I have read that the BLT HQ slept 300 Marines. I don't
know exactly how many were inside when the truck exploded,
but [I] suspect most of them were inside, given the number who
died. I know the Navy sailors bunked there as well.[2]

Nothing like this had ever made the morning news. We were all
watching in disbelief. Everyone in the lobby knew my brother was over
there. I talked about him all the time. He would send me funny letters,
and after ripping into those letters at the campus post office I would
share his stories with my freshmen friends.

I would get so excited to receive letters from Mecot. His sense of humor was ridiculously silly. He always joked about my schedule. When I
sent him a letter and told him I was taking horseback riding he replied,
"What next, sis, underwater basket weaving? Ha!" Mecot had a great
ability to make people laugh, especially me! Only my American brother
would come up with underwater basket weaving.

So there I was, in the lobby of Belk Dorm watching footage of the af-
termath of the bombing. At that point I was surrounded by my friends,
who were a great sense of comfort to me. They kept reassuring me he
was OK. I suddenly did not feel alone or away from family. And of
course, I did not want to accept the possibility that my only brother may
have just been killed.

It was undoubtedly horrifying. Where was my brother in all the rubble? The news footage was graphic and gruesome. I kept looking for
him on the television. Was he alive? Who did this? Why? So many
questions—whom could I look to for answers? I ran down the hallway
back to my dorm room and called home, realizing later that Mom was

[2] Reprinted with permission from Edward S. Marek, Lt. Col., U.S.AF (Ret.), "Largest Non-Nuclear Explosion on Record Hits Beirut Marines, Twenty-Five Years Ago," Talking Proud (October 2008), available at http://www.talkingproud.us/Retired/Retired/BeirutMarines.html.

already at Camp Lejeune visiting Mecot's wife, Tammy, who is also known as "Rat," and their seventeen-month-old son, named Mecot Echo.

Mecot and Tammy spent endless hours trying to come up with a baby name they liked for a girl or a boy. As it turned out, according to Tammy, on a snowflake-filled winter night while she and Mecot were snuggling in our log cabin at Canaan Valley Ski Resort, they heard a coyote in the distance and it was actually echoing. She said they looked at each other and both said Echo. They laughed and knew that was it meant to be. They both loved the name and it would always hold that special moment in time.

4

Call to Duty

I N 1980, AFTER ONE YEAR OF COLLEGE, MECOT felt a restlessness that would lead him on a different path. His classes didn't interest him. However, he loved his fraternity brothers, the mixers and the charity work they did. He loved the brotherhood but often wondered if there was something more that he was called to do in his life.

He would spend a lot time at "the farm." The farm was the tract of land that Daddy had bought for him so that when he got married he could build a house there and be close to the family. It was halfway between Concord College (where Mecot attended freshman year) in Athens, West Virginia, and our home in Hinton.

We had that tract of land for a while. Daddy purchased it when I was just a toddler. He wanted somewhere that the family could go on the weekends to get away from daily life and enjoy the outdoors together. We would go there as a family and hike around the woods, target shoot empty milk bottles, play cards, and just hang out.

As we got older, Mecot would drive his jeep, Rover, down the very long and narrow road to the farm and have a few beers and think. That was his thinking spot. So Mecot went there one morning rather than attending class at Concord College.

It was there he felt his call to duty among the peacefulness of the trees in the fields, the dew-covered grass, and the continuously flowing hills.

He wanted to make a difference in this world and he knew how important it was to live in a country with freedom. Growing up with patri-

Mecot, Daddy, and me at our farm in Pipestem. Mecot stands fearless with his gun while I cling to Daddy. The loud sound it made echoing off the mountains scared me.

otic parents, one homegrown from Lexington, Kentucky (with a family history of uncles serving in our Navy), and one from the struggling country of the Philippines (with a history of family taking refuge in the mountains from the Japanese during World War II), he had learned to value our country and everything it stood for. He had that character about him. Everyone who came in contact with him knew him as a young man with a drive to succeed and help others.

Surrounded by the tranquility of the mountains, he knew at that moment that his calling was to serve our country and become a United States Marine.

So he drove away from tranquility and ended up in the commotion of our neighboring town of Beckley. Beckley was the big metropolis compared to our small, diminishing railroad town of Hinton. He parked Rover and proceeded into the U.S. Marine enlistment office. No one was forcing him to enlist, other than his own heart and soul calling him to serve our country. He completed the paperwork and testing. He was, however, slightly concerned because of his missing toe tips (more on the missing toe tips later), but luckily for him it did not create an issue for rejection. It was almost comical, because the enlisting officer did not quite believe the "missing toe tips" written on his application form. But after Mecot took off his shoes, the officer understood. Once everything was completed, he proceeded to load back up in Rover and head down the mountain to tell the family.

The cool, crisp fall air coming down the mountainside and blowing through our kitchen windows could not stop the breathlessness our family felt while Mecot stood proudly and gingerly as he told us he had joined the U.S. Marines. He was leaving in a few weeks. It was very difficult for all of us, most especially our parents. He was the only son in the family and the pride and joy for us and our little town. What little did we know that his devotion to his country would take him away from all of us.

5

Heading Home

As I was dialing Tammy, a girlfriend from my dorm said a gentleman was on the hall phone for me. He said it was urgent. Every one of my hall mates stood with their heads leaning out their doors, watching and listening in anticipation of my reaction to the phone call. All of them stood in fear.

I received the news from a family friend back home in Hinton that Mecot was one of the first pulled from the rubble, and for half a second I thought he meant that Mecot had been pulled free, alive. But something in my heart instinctively felt otherwise. I could tell by the sound of my friend's voice, who then told me very matter-of-factly that he did not survive.

So when I received the phone call from home, Tammy had just found out a few minutes before me. It took only a matter of minutes before the news reporters were knocking at her apartment door. My mom was visiting her at the time. Mom opened the door, only to have the microphone shoved into her face with the cameras rolling. The news reporter identified himself and asked if Tammy was home and what was her reaction. My mother gave him the "stare."

The stare meaning, if you could have read her mind, "How dare you? How could you? My son has just been killed, my daughter-in-law is in shock, my grandson is screaming right along with his mama, and you want an interview?" She did say, "Do not ever knock on this door again, and tell every one of your reporter friends to stay away." And with that said, she slammed the door shut.

Back at school, I immediately grabbed my purse and car keys. All I wanted was to go home. As I was running and screaming hysterically out the door, I saw two U.S. Marines in their dress blues. When they saw me, they continued walking with calmness, dignity, and respect. They were walking side by side as if marching in cadences. I had been informed by my family friend that if a U.S. Marine were killed, a Marine would convey the death in person to his family members. He told me to expect them to visit.

They came through our front doors and sat down with me and told me that Mecot was killed, though I already knew it. He was one of the first to be identified; his body was intact and easily distinguishable. They were sending him home as expeditiously as possible for burial.

I tried to keep my composure. I was a Camara, as Mecot used to remind me, and we were a strong family. I listened to them with great respect and understanding. I thanked them and then I just lost it. I immediately drove my little VW Rabbit home. I didn't know where to go other than home, my small town in Hinton, where I grew up with my brother, my hero.

Halfway home on I-77, I saw flashing lights in my rearview mirror. The police pulled me over in Virginia and said that an APB had been issued on me. My family had heard I'd left the dorm in anguish and was worried where I'd gone. I was beyond hysterical at that point. The police knew what had happened to my brother, but they didn't understand or have any answers for me as I sat there clinging to the steering wheel and screaming "Why?" You could hear my screams echoing from the mountains.

They kindly asked me to follow them to the police station so that I could calm down, and then they would lead me home. I did as asked. They gave me a warm beverage and crackers and tried to console me as best as possible. They were in disbelief. I was in shock. And the world seemed to be standing still, waiting for resolve.

In the attack on the American Marines barracks, the death toll was 241 American servicemen: 220 Marines, 18 sailors, and three Army soldiers, along with sixty Americans injured, representing the deadliest single-day death toll for the United States Marine Corps since the Battle of Iwo Jima of World War II, the deadliest single-day death toll for the United States military since the first day of the Tet Offensive during the Vietnam War, and the deadliest single attack on Americans overseas since World War II. ...The explosives used were equivalent to 5,400 kg (12,000 pounds) of TNT.[3]

Suicide bombing was not a common or anticipated weapon of war in 1983. For 241 of these military personnel, their "duty to serve" as peacekeepers was now transformed into the all too familiar funeral adage "may they rest in peace."

I eventually calmed down at the Virginia State Troopers office and an officer escorted me all the way to the West Virginia state line. He was driving the speed limit with his siren lights spinning. He slowed down and flashed on the rotating red lights atop his police car, then admirably saluted to me as he drove off. With the saddest frown that has ever projected from my face, I waved good-bye and mouthed the words thank you.

I crossed the West Virginia line, driving in a daze through the harvest-colored mountains. Although that day the mountains felt cold, rugged, and gray to me. The leaves, with their gorgeous Indian-summer hues, were just starting to drop, and there was a cold chill that afternoon.

I drove past Concord College in Athens, where Mecot attended school for a short while. I drove through Pipestem, where Mecot hunted and fished at our hunting camp. I drove past Bluestone Lake, where Mecot sat up his summer tent and camped and fished for weeks at a time dur-

---

[3] *Wikipedia*, s.v. "1983 Beirut barracks bombing," last modified April 30, 2013, http://en.wikipedia.org /wiki/1983_Beirut_barracks_bombing.

ing the summer months. All I saw was Mecot and his smirky grin imprinted everywhere in these mountains.

Down the road from our home stands proudly the statue of John Henry. Some of you might know his legend, but some of you might not. ...I now equate my brother's legendary status with that of John Henry.

In a nutshell, "John Henry's heroism is associated with several elements: his strength and grit as a working-class common man, his status as a hero to African American laborers, and his allegorical depiction of 'the tragedy of man versus machine.'"[4]

According to *Wikipedia*, "In almost all versions of the story, John Henry is a black man of exceptional physical gifts, a former slave, possibly born in Tennessee. Henry becomes the greatest 'steel-driver' in the mid-nineteenth-century push to expand railroads from the east coast of the United States, across and through the mountains, to the frontier West. However, the owner of the railroad buys a steam-powered hammer to do the work of his mostly black steel-driving crew. To save his job and the jobs of his men, John Henry challenges the owner to a contest: Henry will race the steam-powered hammer."[5] John Henry beats the machine, but exhausted, he collapses and dies.

John Henry was a hero. He died fighting for a cause. He wanted to save his job and the jobs of his men—a cause that meant something to him and his community. Mecot, my American brother, was a hero too. He died fighting for a cause—a cause to protect and defend our country and our country's international interests. His duty was to be a peacekeeper for an unstable nation.

That's all I could think about while driving the last stretch home. I neared our driveway and put the blinker on my VW Rabbit and turned up the long bumpy hillside. Mecot, my big brother, my only brother, would never be home again. My tears were streaming down my face just

---

[4] *Wikipedia*, s.v. "John Henry (folklore)," last modified March 3, 2013, http://en.wikipedia.org/wiki/John_Henry_%28folklore%29.
[5] Ibid.

like Daddy's long cascading waterfall in our gardens. As I approached the door, there was no one home except our priest, Father Paul Tedesco, and my Aunt Era. The Virginia Highway Patrol had notified them that I would be there shortly.

I made it through the front door and collapsed in our family room beneath the statue of Jesus. Daddy had adorned almost every room with a religious statue. He always told us that he was going to be a priest in the Philippines but was sent to America to become a successful doctor to help provide for the rest of the family. He knew he wanted to help others one way or another, and this way he could also help his family and send money home to support his seventeen siblings. Yes, seventeen siblings. And yes, he went back to the Philippines regularly and helped provide for his family there as well.

Father Paul and Aunt Era found me screaming hysterically—as if someone had just stabbed me in the heart—and crying to Daddy, Jesus, and every saint I could think of to please tell me it was a huge mistake. He's alive. He has to be. He's my only brother. He would never leave me. They found me curled up in a ball on the floor below the statue of Jesus. Aunt Era insisted that I drink just a little orange juice to help me calm down. I remember nothing from that point on until a day and a half later.

I woke up in my pink lace and linen canopy bed complete with silky-soft sheets that felt like rose petals. I sat up in a complete daze. My sister and my aunts came in just as I was sitting up. I uttered, "Where's Mecot?" My Aunt Era with a very soft, saddened tone of voice said he had definitely been identified as one of the Marines that did not make it out alive and that his body would be home in a few days. Oh my God! Oh my God! I started getting worked up all over again. Then Aunt Era told me to take deep breaths. With tears building up in her big brown eyes, she told me she had crushed up two sleeping pills in my orange juice to calm me. She and Father Paul tried relentlessly for forty-five minutes to console me and nothing was working. You need to start working through this. Take deep breaths. We are all here. And I said,

"Yes, except my big brother: the most amazing big brother in the world. When do I get to see him?"

My sister and aunt helped me climb out of bed, wash my face, and walk down our hallway, past Mecot's bedroom (I could not even look in it), past our kitchen, and into our family room. We called that room the "orange room" because it had bright orange shag carpet that Mom and Dad fell in love with.

Our family, friends, and neighbors sat glued to the monstrous-screen TV, viewing ABC's World News Tonight with Peter Jennings. Mom and Tammy watched and sobbed buckets of tears while keeping a careful ear for the telephone call from the Marine Corps advising when Mecot would be home.

Our very large TV sat caddy corner to our fireplace, and we were one of the few homes that could afford cable TV at the time. It was a new concept but taking off quickly. We had "the box" that we had to walk up to in order to change the channels. Remote controls did not exist at that time. The TV was our biggest source of information other than the calls that Mom and Tammy were making nonstop to Camp Lejeune.

Finally, Tammy did receive the call with details. As reported, most of the Marines had still been sleeping. It was 6:00 a.m. The suicide bomber made contact with the BLT headquarters building where Mecot slept.

Mecot was one of the first to be identified because the explosion blew him completely out of the building. His body was not buried under rubble. He was found still alive, extremely battered and bruised with massive head injuries.

Two Marines found him and requested for an immediate chopper to airlift him to the ship where all the injured were being sent. They stayed with him the entire way. They made it to the ship.

But the medical unit was well below the deck and near the very bottom of the ship. They kept yelling for him to hang on: "You're going to be OK! Hang on! Keep fighting; do not stop fighting! You are going to be OK, Sergeant! Do not stop breathing!"

They had almost made it to the medical unit but his breathing was becoming very shallow. His friends screamed one last time, "Damn it, Mecot! Do not stop breathing!" And there, in the tiny dark elevator of the ship, was where Mecot took his last breath. He died from massive head injuries due to the force of the blast.

He was one of the first to be identified since his body was intact. However, it took six long days of waiting before Mecot's body made it back to the States and back home to our small all-American town of Hinton. Mecot loved his hometown of Hinton, West Virginia. He grew into an American hero there.

6

Memorial Day in the Mountains

EMORIAL DAY, MAY 31, 1970. Why were we standing in silence on that bright sunny spring day in May? We were gazing at the colorful wreaths so elegantly decorated with patriotic ribbons blowing in the crisp air. They were hanging from a perfectly created wall made of river rock. The rocks that I'm sure came from the river alongside my home. And it is with these rocks that my brother eventually taught me how to skip stones across the river. But that's another story. He had more skips than anyone I ever met. I did good to skip a stone three times across the river. Mecot once hit seven skips. That's unheard of in these parts.

The river we skipped stones along is called the Greenbrier. It was just down the hill from our home. It converges with the Bluestone River and the New River below our main hometown bridge.

Growing up, I could hear the waves gliding across the river rocks all the time. At night, when I slept with the window open I could hear the river. It would lull me to sleep. And in the morning I would hear the rumble of the trains chugging by. Occasionally the engineer would blow the whistle. I didn't need an alarm on those days.

Our town sat right where the rivers converged. The Bluestone River and the New River met right above the Bluestone Dam.

Anyway, on that particular day, on the perfectly manicured green, green grass, I was standing with my big brother, Mecot. He is five years older than me. Also, I was standing with my sister, Threase. She is seven years older than me. We were standing with my mom and dad. And we were all standing with the rest of the families residing in this little town nestled in a valley where three rivers converge surrounded by gently rolling mountains.

Hinton was created by the coal mining boom of the 1870s. At that time it was established as a major terminal point on the railroad.

Although, as the railroad changed from steam-powered to diesel-powered locomotives, fewer workers and engine crews were required to maintain and operate trains from the Hinton terminal.

During the years that followed, our town's population declined; however, those families that remained were loyal and hardworking. They were determined to keep our town thriving. Their hard work ethic and determination to keep our town alive stemmed from their family lineage of coal miners, railroad operators, and military servicemen and women.

And it was there that my mom and dad decided to raise my brother, my sister, and me. They found a deep respect and loyalty to these people and their heritage of American values and to their generations of families who called Hinton home. My dad grew up with the same values in the Philippines and he felt a sincere connection to the townsfolk of Hinton.

Just two blocks down from the Memorial Park was where my dad's doctor's office was located. That's where he served as chief town doctor and where my mom worked closely beside him as his nurse.

I didn't fully understand the memorial—why it was there, why we were there. I was only five and a half years old at the time. Some people had tears gently rolling down their cheeks. Some were holding pictures. Some were holding each other.

I was holding Daddy's hand. He would look down at me occasionally and kiss my forehead. He reminded me to listen to Father Hickey, our town priest, and to be respectful and loving to those around us.

I was a very inquisitive five-and-a-half-year-old. "Why?" was my favorite question to ask and still is to this day. And after the service, I had to ask my mommy why our friends and family were so sad.

She placed her arm around me while she summoned Mecot and Threase to join us, and we strolled to the park bench that sat facing the memorial wall. The sun was glistening on the metallic engraved names decorated on each wreath. Together we sat down and she softly read to us one of the names on a wreath.

She then told us that the name she read, John McCoy, was the name of a brother, father, and uncle. He was a family member from Hinton. And he was no longer living. He gave his life so that we could be there today with our community, living a life of freedom, safety, and peace. Later in life, I came to understand exactly her sentiment.

But at that moment I was only interested in socializing with my friends at the ice cream stand and chasing the dandelions that were being whisked away from the gentle spring breeze.

It was here, Hinton, West Virginia, a valley nestled in the Appalachian Mountains, that launched the heroic evolution of my American brother. I got to witness, firsthand, what drives an American-raised boy to willingly become an American warrior.

7

Mecot Gets Hooked

W HAT IS THE DEFINITION OF COMRADE? The dictionary defines comrade as "a person who shares in one's activities, occupation, etc.; companion, associate, or friend" and "a fellow member of a fraternal group, political party, etc."[6]

My American brother, Mecot, started at a very early age adhering to the true definition of the word. It began along the mountainside of 1008 Greenbrier Drive, Hinton, West Virginia, our childhood home.

We did not live in a preplanned neighborhood like they have in today's towns and cities. Our neighborhood consisted of homes tucked away in the mountainside or along the riverbank.

It was there along Greenbrier Drive that Mecot became "a fellow member of a fraternal group," "a person who shares in one's activities," and "a friend."

His first comrades were his neighborhood buddies from Greenbrier Drive. Everyone befriended Mecot, or should I say vice versa: Mecot befriended everyone. He never had an enemy growing up. His contagious, happy, friendly, energetic self never stopped until his head hit the pillow every night at bedtime.

So let's talk neighborhood buddies and what began the infamous career of an American brother, a comrade.

[6] *Random House Webster's College Dictionary*, 2nd ed., s.v. "comrade."

Mecot's comrades had painted faces and were dressed in military boots, helmets, and camouflage pants and shirts. I felt like I was living on a military base at times. There was Keith Foster, Keith Graham, Jackie Scott, and Don Williams, to name a few. They would create the most elaborate battle scenes from inside our home to outside along the mountainside or riverbanks. Creativity and imagination began at a young age in our neighborhood. It flowed like the brisk waters of the Greenbrier River, constantly moving and constantly changing. Those buckets of army men were everywhere!

I felt like I was constantly walking onto a battlefield. And if I accidentally trampled onto the battle zone, I was graciously escorted away by real-life military commandos. Did I say commandos or comrades?

I would whine in sheer agony: "Ouch, Nanny! I can't take it!" It was painful stepping on those plastic, well-defined army men that Mecot would set up all over the house.

Every day was a new day on the battlefront for Mecot and his comrades. When they were done battling and bonding with the little plastic warriors, they would always move on to more adventures.

For example, living along the river and having a father of Filipino descent from a fishing family, Mecot learned quickly to love the art of fishing. He and his neighborhood comrades often fished along the riverbanks. Whatever they would catch, my father would clean and grill the same evening. His fishing adventures usually ended with a great yummy dinner of grilled fish, rice, and fresh vegetables from the neighbor's garden. And almost always, our dinner conversations were centered on Mecot's incredible story of how the big one got away.

But there was one day that he did not come back with a line full of fresh fish or the infamous big one got away story!

What made that day's fishing adventure so different from any other? It was a blue-sky, sweltering-summer-heat kind of day. Mecot and Keith Foster decided it was a good day to go fishing off the riverbank and cool off. It was always a little cooler along the riverbank. There were lots of big shade trees and cool river rock to perch on. There you could stick your feet in the water, cast a fishing line, and feel that nice swift flow of cool water chilling you down.

They grabbed some bait and two Cokes from Skidmore's Bait Shop. Mr. and Mrs. Skidmore owned this little shop and just loved when the neighborhood boys would come in.

Mecot would help Mrs. Skidmore occasionally with the bait. He would separate out the worms and crawdaddies into containers for her. Mrs. Skidmore's smile and humble appreciativeness melted Mecot's heart. He never asked to be paid and when they offered he refused their money. Mecot instinctively learned from an early age what it meant to help people whenever possible.

So once they loaded up with bait and their Cokes they strutted across Greenbrier Drive and onto the riverbank. Mecot exclaimed, "Keith, it's a good day for fishing! I know we're going to hit the jackpot today. And who knows, I might just catch the Big One!" Keith responded with affirmation, "Yep, today's the day, bro! You and me and a big catch, that's what I'm talking about."

Keith sucked down a few sips of Coke and baited his hook with a squirmy worm. No sooner had he cast back his line than he hooked Mecot in the head! Yes, his squirmy wormed hook just caught the biggest fish of all. That would be Mecot.

The big hook settled deep in the top of his head. It was painful and Mecot wasn't particularly happy. Usually nothing got to Mecot, but this definitely did. "Holy hell! Did you just hook my head? Get it out now, dude!" Mecot asserted. After Keith had offered his expert medical evaluation and opinion, it was determined that the hook wasn't coming out on its own or with Dr. Keith's unskilled hands.

Mecot was never one to panic, but he was very upset and in pain at that point; moreover, Keith was in shock and freaking out that he'd hooked his friend's head. But Mecot's leadership skills came through.

"Keith, help me out, bro. You carry the pole and walk behind me and keep that line loose, and let's head to the hospital." Luckily, it was just up the road about a half mile and Mecot knew that's where Daddy was going to be. "Dad will get the hook out with his medical tools. So walk slowly and stop freaking out!" Keith was exercising extreme caution while trying desperately to stop shaking.

But he was shaking so much the fishing pole was moving and tugging on Mecot's head.

Mecot shouted, "Stop shaking, Keith! Calm down; you're driving it farther into my head! It's OK, dude. Just keep walking." Keith calmed down and both of them climbed off the river rocks very carefully, drudged up the riverbank onto Greenbrier Drive, and slowly tramped alongside the road all the way to the hospital. They eventually made it. Keith walked very carefully into the emergency room, with Mecot in agony at this point and Keith trying to do everything to not make the pole shake. He did not want to upset the new patient.

All the hospital staff knew he was Dr. Camara's son, and so they immediately called for Daddy to come to the emergency room. It was the most excitement the ER had seen in weeks. It was like a three-ring circus, with staff coming out of the woodwork to witness Dr. Camara's son with a fishhook in the head. Everyone remained calm, although some of the nurses could not help but laugh a little. So did Daddy, after he removed the hook, of course.

Mecot's embarrassment soon turned to stardom as all the young candy-stripe volunteers strolled by, smiling and letting him know that they were available should he need anything at all.

Keith, on the other hand, received the cold shoulder from the candy-stripe volunteers as they shook their heads and gestured shame on you. He sat there like a sad clown the whole time. He tried to wink at the girls and explain it was an accident, but they just kept walking down the corridor.

However, he did not leave Mecot's side during the entire procedure to remove the hook. He was right there as Daddy and the nurse carefully extracted it. Keith was a true comrade too, a faithful friend.

So Mecot ended up with about twelve stitches on his head, a fishhook in a jar as a keepsake, cute candy stripers ready to nurse him back to health, and a hospital staff that made him feel like a prince. They all loved and respected our father so much, and as a result they loved Mecot like one of their own as well.

That day was a true test of brotherhood for him and Keith. And like a true warrior, he remained calm—albeit very bothered by the whole incident—and loyal to Keith. They ended up walking all the way home together. Keith made sure Mecot got home all right, and Mecot made sure Keith knew that their friendship could endure anything…even a fishhook to the head!

Daddy and Mecot at the Bluestone Dam with big smiles.
Obviously, they're happy with their big catch of the day, 1974.

8

High School Days: 1974-1979

THE TEENAGE YEARS WERE A GREAT TIME of adventure and growth for Mecot. We were blessed to grow up in a very, very small town in West Virginia. We were somewhat isolated from global happenings, unless they directly affected one of our own townspeople. And then, of course, we all felt the suffering and came together for support. If one of the townsfolk had a family member involved in any military action, we would all know about it. And we would all be supportive to that family in whatever manner they needed.

My father taught us at an early age to love unconditionally, to not judge people based on their belongings but to respect them for their family values and to always make others feel loved.

As a result, my mother incorporated those values into our daily lives as the Vietnam War escalated. We each had a POW/MIA bracelet that we wore every day with the name of one of our U.S. soldiers imprinted on it. My sister, brother, and I were very young at the time. However, our mom and dad took the time to explain the importance of each of the men on our wrist, and the importance of praying for their safe return when we said our prayers at night. Every night our family came together in the hallway of our home; my father had created a beautiful alcove in the hallway with the statue of Saint Joseph at the end. We would kneel together and pray as a family. During this time, we always prayed for world peace and the safe return of all our American troops.

Our family photo from our annual Christmas Party, 1975.

We were taught that the names on our bracelets were American troops in a terrible situation defending our freedoms, and that we must pray for each of them and appreciate their sacrifices. We all listened very intently as we were told about the bracelets. Mecot, of course, had a glistening blank stare. Looking back, I can see he felt a deep connection to what these troops were doing in order for us to live a life of freedom. Those bracelets meant very much to each of us. And as for Mecot, he felt a sense of calling, because our mother always said they represented someone special and that they were not just names imprinted on a piece of metal. It was someone's father or brother whom we needed to pray for, for a safe return from their military service and devotion. They had been risking their lives every day to make our country better, stronger, and more united in the pursuit for world peace and freedom for all.

At the time I did not fully understand how a bracelet could mean so much. But later I learned that the idea originated from two young ladies who wanted something tangible that would be a way to remember those Americans who served our country and had not returned home safely. As quoted by Carol Bates Brown,

> ...the idea for the bracelets was started by college student Kay Hunter and me, as a way to remember American prisoners of war suffering in captivity in Southeast Asia. In late 1969, television personality Bob Dornan (who several years later was elected to the U.S. Congress) introduced us and several other members of VIVA [Voices In Vital America] to three wives of missing pilots. They thought our student group could assist them in drawing public attention to the prisoners and missing in Vietnam. The idea of circulating petitions and letters to Hanoi demanding humane treatment for the POWs was appealing, as we were looking for ways college students could become involved in positive programs to support U.S. soldiers without becoming embroiled in the controversy of the war itself.

On Veterans Day, November 11, 1970, the official bracelet program was kicked off at the Universal Sheraton Hotel. Public response quickly grew and we eventually got to the point we were receiving over 12,000 requests a day. This also brought money in to pay for brochures, bumper stickers, buttons, advertising, and whatever else we could do to publicize the POW/MIA issue. We formed a close alliance with the relatives of missing men. They got bracelets from us on consignment and could keep some of the money they raised to fund their local organizations. We also tried to furnish these groups with all the stickers and other literature they could give away.

We ended up dropping out of college to work for VIVA full time to administer the bracelet and other POW/MIA programs—none of us got rich off the bracelets. VIVA's adult advisory group, headed by Gloria Coppin, was adamant that we would not have a highly paid professional staff. As I recall, the highest salary was $15,000 a year and we were able to keep administrative costs to less than 20 percent of income.

In all, VIVA distributed nearly five million bracelets and raised enough money to produce untold millions of bumper stickers, buttons, brochures, matchbooks, newspaper ads, etc., to draw attention to the missing men. In 1976, VIVA closed its doors. By then the American public was tired of hearing about Vietnam and showed no interest in the POW/MIA issue.[7]

The three of us always wore these bracelets. I am surprised Mecot did not lose his through all his teenage adventures. And it was these adventures that nurtured the warrior in him at an early age. My American brother was emerging before my very eyes, one adventure at a time.

---

[7] Carol Bates Brown, "History of the POW/MIA Bracelets," MIA Facts Site, http://www.miafacts.org/bracelets.htm. Reprinted with permission.

What follows is a little collection of Mecot's adventures that groomed him for the life of a United States Marine.

First, there came the very frightening tale that I have nicknamed "John Boat, Jerry, and the Great Flood!" Mecot and his best friend, Jerry Berry, decided to take a john boat down the rapidly rising flood waters of the Greenbrier River, directly in front of our street where our house was nestled along the mountainside. Since the street was completely submerged, Mecot concluded that it was a once in a lifetime opportunity that they could not pass up: paddling down a street that was normally congested with traffic heading back and forth from downtown to the countryside. The headline for the next day's *Hinton News* was GREEN- BRIER RIVER HITS FLOOD STAGE RECORD; moreover, the story also incor- porated a photo of Mecot and Jerry, with smiles so big you could see

News photo of Mecot and Jerry briskly drifting down the flooded Greenbrier River. Notice that they do not have boat oars: Mecot has a piece of driftwood and Jerry has a shovel.

their pearly whites from across the embankment, as well as Mecot's great tale of his paddling a john boat through floodwaters. But that's not the end of the story. Little did Mecot know that the water was eight feet above flood stage and moving extremely fast, and that all the neighbors watching were completely frightened for the boys' safety. Luckily, a few trees had fallen into the river but had not been swept away, and they managed to frantically paddle over to one of them, grab hold, and swiftly paddle to the embankment, where they jumped out. Mecot made sure Jerry made it up first. He had a deep loyalty to his friends at all times; even in the middle of a raging flood he wanted Jerry to be safe first!

Second and even more frightening is the adventure that I call "Lawn Mower Mayhem." Mecot was always helpful and never, ever complained about doing chores, especially mowing the lawn. I think he thought it was a very macho, grown-up task for a teenage boy to take on, and he welcomed any chore that had to do with him being outside while being manly. He was definitely known to live outside more than inside. He could spend weeks during the summer living in his tent along the lake. "Bonding with the wilderness" is what he would tell Mom and Dad when they asked why he wasn't coming home to his warm, comfy bed.

So that particular spring morning, he got up and decided to tackle the lawn first thing. Now, springtime in the mountains is usually sunny; but it's cool in the mornings with an immense collection of dewdrops. His smart thinking told him to do it in the morning before it got too hot and before his neighborhood comrades gathered at our home to formulate a game plan for their day's outdoor adventures. Usually in the spring, their plans would range from fishing to tennis to throwing canoes in one of the three rivers and heading downstream. That particular morning was much different. That particular morning was life changing.

He climbed out of bed. He ate his regular giant bowl of Frosted Flakes. It was his favorite, favorite cereal and he would always joke about Tony the Tiger. He would imitate him by standing on his chair at the table and stretching up and roaring, "THEY'RE GRRREAT!"

So after his Frosted Flakes fuel, Mecot decided to start the mowing process behind the house, directly along the mountainside.

It was a very, very steep slope. Mecot cranked up the old mower and was ready to go at it. As he was holding on to the lawn mower and heading down the hillside, his right foot slipped underneath the mower from the wet dew.

He released the lawn mower, fell alongside the hill, and gazed at the blood pouring through his half-cut Converse high-top tennis shoes. He ran into the house screaming in agony, "I chopped off my foot! I chopped off my foot! Help! Help!" It was a Saturday morning and Daddy had just finished his rounds at the hospital. Daddy thought he was home to work in the garden, but little did he know he was heading back to the hospital with Mecot.

Mecot was still screaming in pain as Mom and Dad loaded him into the car. His neighborhood buddies were just coming to the house when they heard him screaming. They ran down the hillside where our home set nestled close to the base of the mountain and within feet of the river. Frantically, they must have asked me twenty questions about what happened to Mecot. I told them that he'd chopped off his foot when he was mowing the lawn and Dad and Mom were rushing him to the ER. Daddy did not examine or touch his foot until they made it to the ER. Mecot was in too much pain.

His friends ran up the hill, climbed onto their bikes, and pedaled faster than I'd ever seen anyone go on a bike.

They were racing to meet him at the hospital. We had a back mountain road that led straight to the hospital. It was only about two miles away. They biked into that hospital parking lot and straight to the front door. They busted through those doors and headed straight to the ER. His fellow comrades were there standing by his side. It took a couple hours to work on Mecot's foot. My mom kept coming out to keep his friends, my sis, my aunts, and me informed.

I asked, "Mommy, please don't tell me he cut off his foot." You could have heard a pin drop. His friends were pacing silently, my two aunts were silently praying their rosary, and my big sis was holding my hand to settle me.

Mom, calm yet concerned, told us his foot was not cut off but he might lose a few toes. I really did not feel much better about that. We waited and waited.

Finally, Daddy came out with an exhausted look and told us Mecot did not cut off his foot, but he had lost the tips of his big toe and second toe. Daddy said he should have a full recovery; however, he was somewhat concerned about his balance when walking and running, but we'd take it one day at a time.

Daddy waited until Mecot woke up from surgery and calmly told him about the loss of his toe tips. He accepted the loss of his toe tips admirably. And not too long after he was out of his hospital bed, he was slowly putting weight back on his foot. He practiced walking a lot, pacing the hospital hallway back and forth. We all took turns walking with him.

His friends did not leave his side that day. They stayed with him until it was getting dark, and then they rode their bikes back to the neighborhood and home for the evening. They came back each day until he was released from the hospital a few days later.

By the summer, his toes were completely healed. The loss of his toe tips did not slow him down at all. His balance was intact and he was moving on to his next teenage adventure.

Growing up in a small American town really made Mecot a strong, brave, kindhearted U.S. Marine. He valued every day that he could be outdoors living in peace and harmony with the mountains and the river. He realized and respected this freedom so much and never took it for granted.

This brings me to his third little adventure. He loved being on the river. Mecot was hired by Richie Cantrell, an expert river expedition guide, to work during the summers as a guide for river expeditions. He felt a deep respect for the river perhaps because his life was not taken during "John Boat, Jerry, and the Great Flood."

It was during a practice rafting downstream that something magical happened to Mecot. Mecot was a great storyteller, and he used to tell the story like this: "The waves were pounding down around me and as the sun was beating down upon my big burly body the heavens opened up and caught my soul on fire!" At that moment, he was transformed into a tribal Indian from the Wauhatchie tribe. He called himself the Last of the Wauhatchie. He was very proud of his calling. He said that he carried with him the tough, high-spirited, brave traits that make him pure Wauhatchie. The Wauhatchie Indian tribe may have been completely unreal, but for me, for the townsfolk of Hinton, and for all his rafting customers, we completely bought into the idea. (I found out later that in reality, "Wauhatchie" was the name of a Cherokee chieftain.)

Mecot would make it very clear to the tourists he took down the river that he was one with the river because he was the Last of the Wauhatchie Indians. I remember being at the rafting center when the tourists came back, and boy were they talking about their tour guide. Mecot always assured his guests that they were in good hands and there was nothing to fear. And he always promised them a safe passage through the waters and a safe return from the river journey. He was very convincing and he never lost a rafter to the river!

Today, if you go rafting with Cantrell River Expeditions, there is one raft that has Mecot's name in huge letters along the side. When cars go by along the riverside, his name is clearly discernible on that large raft. Richie, the owner, wanted to memorialize Mecot. No better way than to have his spirit imprinted on one of the rafts.

His next adventure happened during that same summer. In summertime, Hinton always hosted the West Virginia Water Festival. It was a huge event for the state and, most especially, our town. Events such as the downtown parade and firemen's parade were held as well as the festival coronation and boat races.

We had speedboaters from all over the world come to participate on the stunning Bluestone Lake for the boating competition. That was the main event, followed closely by the crowning of the queen. It was a huge production. A floating stage was erected near the Bluestone Dam, with all the princesses from each county strolling, singing, and dancing while local judges selected who would be queen. Mecot thoroughly enjoyed this event.

We were blessed to have a lovely home that hosted an annual Water Festival luncheon for all the princesses. Daddy was the world's best host. Everyone always left our home feeling welcome, joyful, and special. Mecot was always very boisterous at these events, as were all his neighborhood comrades. They would put on their best church clothes and strut around our gardens, gazing at the beauty that surrounded them. They always had a contest as to which one of them could get the most autographed pictures of the princesses. It was not every day that they were surrounded by the sheer bliss of pretty girls to dream about.

The festival always held an annual canoe race, starting at the Bluestone Dam and going all the way down to the Bypass. It was this particular year that Mecot decided to enter him and me in the two-man canoe race.

It was a bright, sunny day. The rapids on the New River were perfect. You could hear the rumble of the waves and see the whitecaps from the riverbank. Mecot was completely pumped up to win the race. He was convinced that we had superior skills to win. It was on that day that Mecot made me an honorary Wauhatchie Indian. I knew that meant I was going to have to put out all my muscle for this win.

All the canoes and participants lined up at the base of the Bluestone Dam. As we walked our canoe out, my toes curled up in my Converse sneakers and the water was a bit chilly. But I didn't dare mention that to Mecot. We were in it for the win. I was not going to disappoint my fearless leader. It was that day he looked at me before the starting horn blew and shouted over the rapids, "Congratulations! You are now an honorary member of the tribe, a great li'l sister too."

That really got me fired up! I could not disappoint him no matter what. I was now an official honorary member of the Wauhatchie Indian tribe.

The starting horn blew and we jumped into the canoe. He was in the back and I was in the front. He was belting commands: "Stroke, dig, stroke faster, faster." I had never paddled so hard in my life! He was always driven to succeed in whatever task was at hand. He wanted first place whatever it took. And he never, ever gave up.

We were in the lead until the last quarter of the race. Our canoe had filled with water from the rapids, and Mecot could not bail it out as quickly as it came in.

To the right was Miss Beth—a princess, or so she thought. She was sitting like a queen in the front. She hardly even paddled, and there I was beside her with my arms moving faster than I thought humanly possible for a thirteen-year-old girl.

It was apparent that she and her partner did not have as much water in their canoe slowing them down. They were just cutting through the rapids so calm and agile.

She really was not doing a thing other than sitting there looking like a princess. She had a partner who was simply relentless in his paddling abilities. His abilities, combined with less water in their canoe, gave them an advantage.

My brother never gave up. The front tips of our canoes were even, and we were nearing the end of the race. Mecot was chanting out cadences: "Stroke, stroke; faster, faster!"

The princess ended up jumping in front of us by just a little bit. It was so close. As they crossed the finish line, she looked over at me with the nastiest, most conceited, most arrogant smile my eyes had ever looked upon. I just wanted to take that full bailing bucket and dump it all over her. She did not have a lick of sweat dripping anywhere, and she was hardly even wet. Mecot knew I wanted to let her have it.

I kept looking back at Mecot, telling him I was so sorry. I felt completely to blame for coming in second. He never showed his disappointment. He calmly told me that there was nothing we could do about the amount of water that filled our canoe. We could only bail so much so fast.

We flipped the canoe and then carried it over our heads to the river-bank. Of course, the princess did not assist her partner at all. She steadily walked over the rolling rapids that were knee deep and onto the riverbank while stroking her lipstick around her obnoxious little grin.

I still wanted to throw a bucket of river water all over her face. But Mecot kept me in check. He put his arm around me and walked up to the stage where the winners were presented trophies.

We placed second. He kept his head held high as we received our medals. He whispered that he was proud of me. He was still thrilled to have placed second. He put his arm around me after our medals were placed around our necks and looked at me with sheer gladness to have competed in the race together. He later told me that he was proud to be standing by me and not the wannabe princess. He said I was the real Indian princess, initiated into the Wauhatchie tribe during the canoe race.

Every day was an adventure, and everyone grew more and more to love Mecot for his gregarious personality, his smirky grin, and his sense of commitment to help, protect, and serve those around him.

His high school years were packed with legendary stories to those still living in Hinton. If you ever venture to our small town, mention Mecot's name to anyone and they will have a story to share. Watching him grow up from a little boy to a young man in high school to a U.S. Marine ser-geant, the people of Hinton came to adore him and do even to this day.

<hr />

One of his most memorable high school stories is "Mecot and the Mo-hawk Madness." What better way to intimidate the opposing football team than by marching out on the field two by two, carrying your hel-mets by your hip, arm muscles flexed, standing tall with highly notice-able Mohawk haircuts on each player's head. Mecot had convinced the entire team that this fear factor was just what they needed to win the championship. He was a complete advocate of brotherhood: all for one and one for all. And he always earned the respect of his peers. He gave

Mecot (*center, kneeling*) and the Hinton High School football team leaving the barbershop after they all shaved their heads, ready to intimidate the enemy on the field.

them his undivided attention when they would have something to say, and in turn, his peers would listen to his suggestions and just about one hundred percent of the time would follow his ideas. He was highly motivating and highly convincing.

His great leadership skills and ability to convince anyone of anything worked! Every player on the team had gone to the local barbershop and one by one buzzed his hair into a Mohawk. It was the talk of the town and it made the headlines in the *Hinton News*. And center stage in the newspaper photo was none other than the town sweetheart, Mecot. He had influenced the team to shave their heads before the season started.

High school football was big in West Virginia. It was particularly big in Hinton. The entire town always rallied around the team. Hinton High School football was a town event from pep rallies to booster club events to bake sales to game time. The majority of the town was in full support all season long and most certainly on game nights. The stands would be packed to watch the Hinton Bobcats play under the big lights. The field was built right along the river, and in the evenings Mother Nature's air conditioner cranked on, with the cool river water flowing just feet away from the bleachers. While hot chocolate was always in big demand with the cheerleaders on these chilly nights, the football players would be anything but chilled. They were completely fired up, with sweat collecting at the base their helmets.

It was the following year, in 1978, that the Hinton Bobcats beat Greenbrier West (our arch rival) for homecoming. Greenbrier West were undefeated and ranked fourth in the state. It was a huge win for our small-town high school football boys. The Bobcats never made the playoffs, but they pulled off a great upset at homecoming nonetheless. The entire town was abuzz with excitement! Shaved heads might not have brought on a winning season their junior year, but their senior year proved victorious—shaved heads or not!

Mecot loved, admired, and respected his high school football coach. His name was Bill Garten. He was a very tall, well-built man who spoke in a deep, deep voice. Coach Garten had been the head football coach for years at Hinton High School, and he had taken the Bobcats to many victories. Despite Hinton's declining status of being a railroad metropolis, high school football became the strength and core that kept the townsfolk united. The coaching staff, especially Coach Garten, was always well respected by the players as well as the community.

However, respect was lacking on one particular chilly fall morning. The chill seemed to seep inside the hallway of the old high school. The bell rang to switch classes. As Mecot was passing by in the hall, he encountered a situation and couldn't help but interject his thoughts. He

Mecot's senior high school football
picture, 1979.

was known for speaking his mind quite often when it came to areas of
respect, friendship, and family.

Coach Garten was disciplining a student who was being disruptive in
the hallway. This student had walked out of a class and was bad-
mouthing his teacher, and Coach Garten caught wind of it. Mecot over-
heard this bad-mannered student refer to Coach Garten as "Mr. Garten,"
and he was disrespecting the coach as well. Mecot was quick to correct
him, shouting, "Hey, he has earned the title coach! His name is Coach

Garten, just like my dad earned the title Doctor Camara. My dad was the doctor that reset your broken wrist a few years ago, if I recall correctly. I know you referred to my dad as doctor, and it is exactly the same respect you need to give to Coach Garten. Not Mr. Garten. He has earned his title. You obviously do not like what you're hearing from him, but you still need to be respectful and refer to him as coach from now on. Do you hear me? And knock off the rude comments about your teacher. I know your mama and daddy, and they taught you better than that." Having spoken his mind, Mecot walked away. He looked back at Coach Garten and smiled his smirky grin, adding, "Sorry, Coach. I just had to."

Coach Garten and Mecot shared a special bond. Mecot really looked up to him, not only as a football coach but as a life coach as well. He taught Mecot many things about being a team player and a leader on the field and off.

After my I broke my leg from racing with Mecot on snow skis, I discovered that icy steps just did not work for my abilities with crutches. So for school lunch break every day, Coach Garten and Mecot carried me up and down the steps to Daddy's office, which was just one block from the school.

I truly loved having such a cool big brother in school looking out for me. Mecot genuinely cared for people, especially me, and he always made me feel special. He was never told by my dad or mom to help me with my broken leg. He just did it, although he did ask Coach Garten for his assistance because he was a strong man and happy to be of help .

Not only did Mecot make me feel special as a little sister, but he also made Threase, his big sister, feel special too. He was very protective, always looking out for us. This next little story of brotherhood I titled "Threase and the High School Creep."

Mecot did not like it when boys flirted with us or yelled obscene comments or made rude gestures our way. One day a boy named Ricky Greers (a.k.a. the high school creep) saw Threase walking to Daddy's office after school, and he started yelling some pretty rude, inappropriate comments. He was calling her "super hot" and saying how he'd like to get "a hold of her one day and have his way with her." He tried to catch up with her and started making inappropriate gestures as well.

Mecot just happened to be leaving school in Rover, his jeep, with a few of his football teammates. They were on their way to practice when one of them glanced over and saw what was happening.

Mecot stopped Rover in the middle of the old brick road. He told his fellow teammates to stay in the jeep he would be right back. Of course, his friends wanted to come with him, but he told them to stay in the car, assuring them, "I got this."

Ricky had no idea Mecot was behind him. Threase kept asking him to go home and leave her alone. She was almost to Daddy's office when Mecot tapped Ricky on the shoulder. And with a stern, soft-spoken voice said, "Do not ever speak to my sisters again, and do not ever approach either one of them with your bad manners and ill intentions. Do you hear me?"

Mecot proceeded to knock Ricky's front tooth out, then shouted, "Don't you ever, ever treat anyone like that again. You need to learn some manners and respect for others. Let this be your first lesson in life."

Ricky just stood there in shock, with blood dripping from his mouth and down his chin. His large stature probably kept him anchored and prevented him from falling to the ground. It was at that moment that Daddy came running out of his office, after one of his nurses had told him about the commotion in the street.

Daddy took Ricky in and cleaned up his bloody mouth, then sent him home. Daddy was not particularly happy with Mecot's behavior, but he did feel a sense of relief that Mecot made sure nothing bad happened to Threase.

With a smirky grin of his own, Daddy told Mecot that he could obviously throw a good punch. "Where did you learn to do that?" Daddy asked him. Then he chuckled and went back to his patients.

Mecot's teenage years were full of adventure, camaraderie, and loy-alty. These three elements set the foundation for his transformation later into my American brother, a devoted U.S. Marine.

9

The Fallen Return Home

IT WAS ON OCTOBER 29, 1983, THAT the bodies of fourteen Marines and one sailor killed in Beirut, Lebanon, in the terrorist bombing, arrived at Dover Air Force Base, Delaware. This is the U.S. military's main mortuary. The fallen Marines, the first of the terrorist casualties to return to U.S. soil, were assigned to the Twenty-Fourth Marine Amphibious Unit from Camp Lejeune, North Carolina. The caskets, each draped with an American flag, were arranged in a row inside an aircraft hangar.

All I could think about was that my American brother may be in one of those caskets. His body lay broken and bruised, cold and lifeless. I had been looking forward to his big smirky grin and a big warm bear hug upon his return for the best Thanksgiving feast ever, which would have been in less than one month. But now he was of legendary status: Sgt. Mecot Camara, U.S. Marine, KIA 10-23-83.

I always thought my brother would be famous one day. He had so many qualities that made him exceptional, and the U.S. Marine Corps was more than lucky when he walked through their portal.

He now sits among the ranks of the most elite warriors known to this world. His death and service to his country was acknowledged on November 4, 1983, at a memorial service held at Camp Lejeune. President Reagan and his wife attended the service and afterwards spoke to each of the families of the deceased. I remember sitting between my grieving mother, Mecot's wife Tammy, and their seven-month-old son, Mecot Jr. Tammy was crying inconsolably and holding Mecot Echo as if she would never let go. Tammy was the true love of Mecot's life.

10

How to Love a Rat

I N THE HEART OF DOWNTOWN HINTON at the corner of First Avenue and James Street stands the Summers Memorial Hall. According to the U.S. National Parks Service Registry of Historic Places, the hall was erected in 1938; it is described as a Colonial Revival–style "two-story brick public auditorium building with a temple-form center section flanked by flat-roofed side wings, behind which is an auditorium for public assembly…The interior includes a rotunda extending from the basement through the second story and an imposing auditorium with a balcony and stage and Art Deco lighting."[8]

This building still stands today as prominent a Hinton icon as when originally built. It stands between the Memorial Wall and the courthouse.

Summers Memorial Hall is significant both architecturally and as a major cultural feature within the context of the town, and the building's date stone indicates that it was built "in memory of those who served." Who would have guessed the significance of Mecot meeting his wife in a building dedicated to those who served?

It was during Mecot's high school days that the high school would hold dances for the students in the Memorial Building Auditorium.

---

[8] U.S. Department of the Interior, National Register of Historic Places, "Hinton Historic District (Boundary Revision)," Hinton, Summers County, West Virginia, National Register no. 05000661. Compiled by David L. Taylor. Washington, DC: National Park Service, July 2004. Available at http://www.wvculture.org/shpo/nr/pdf/summers/05000661.pdf.

On one particular cool fall evening, there was a little chill in the air and the stars were like glistening diamonds. Because it was nestled deep in the mountains and away from any big city lights, the stars shined brilliantly in our little town. They projected a picturesque sparkle of the night sky. And the moonlight was just enough to light the way up the grand steps and into the large double doors of the hall.

The high school dance was well underway when a handsome, well-loved, and respected teenager named Mecot and a beautiful, vivacious teenager named Tammy made a connection that would last a lifetime.

Mecot had gone with his friends that evening and, as usual, all the boys were on one side of the room and the girls were on the other.

Mecot had a large gathering of young men around him. He had a way of attracting people to him. He always had a great story to share or an opinion to make known. And he always made sure not to leave anyone out. So on that particular night, Mecot was telling stories about hobbits. He had just started reading *The Hobbit*, and everyone around him was quite intrigued by his talk of hobbits and hobbit life.

Tammy was curious as to why there was a crowd forming there, so she decided to stroll over to see what was happening. She caught a glimpse of this guy telling stories among a circle of fellow students. He caught her eye. He was tall, dark, and handsome with a rather large, smirky grin. She found him very cute, so she decided now was the time to become interested in learning about hobbits too! She remembers that he started staring at her the whole time he was telling his hobbit stories. I know he must have been mesmerized by her beauty and sweetness and also by the fact that she found hobbits interesting. This intrigued him even more.

She told me they began chatting afterward. According to her, their friends kept saying they would make a great couple. Of course, she says, she thought he was the cutest thing ever. Mecot asked her out the very next day and so began their story.

They were the textbook definition of high school sweethearts. She was the gorgeous head majorette in the high school marching band. No

Mecot and Tammy posing before heading out to the
Hinton High School Christmas Dance, 1977.

one could spin a baton like she could. And he was the star football
player, loved for his athletic ability but even more for his ability to lead
his team. He had earned the respect of his teammates and his coaches
early on.

For instance, when the team needed motivation, he got the job done.
When the team needed to be picked up after a loss or pumped up for a
win, his teammates looked up to him to lead. Mecot had an instinctive
ability to lead. His respect by his peers and coaches enabled him to ef-
fortlessly and without hesitation continue to lead in all walks of his life.

Although on that night, it wasn't just his self-proclaimed knowledge
of hobbits and his leadership skills that swept Tammy off her feet. He
never stopped treating her with the tenderness and respect that most
teenage girls give anything to have, and you could see in Tammy's eyes
the complete adoration she had for him.

And let's not forget about the goofiness in their romance. Tammy still
talks about one of her funniest, most romantic moments with Mecot.

Tammy tells it like this:

> OK, this happened when Mecot and I were in tenth grade.
> Mecot and I used to go to Hannah's Floral Shop to eat lunch
> every day. We would walk together from the high school to
> the floral shop, and then when we'd arrive I would get with
> my friends and he would get with his friends to eat. They al-
> ways bugged me and him about why we didn't sit together
> while we ate our lunch. Well, I was just so shy to eat in front
> of him and they all knew this. I look back on it now and think
> of how funny we were about the whole thing. We'd (Mecot
> and I) be sitting across the dining area from each other and
> every so often we'd look to see what the other was doing.
> Each time I saw that he wasn't looking I'd take a bite of my
> food. He'd wave at me or wink at me every now and then.
> We always just laughed about my fear of eating in front of
> him. It was such a big deal to me I would literally get so
> nervous each day at lunchtime—laugh out loud!
>
> Then one day he asked me to go out to eat as he had many
> times in the past. But this certain day all my friends decided
> to gang up on me and push me to go. Well, I felt extremely
> pressured to go ahead and try it. So he set the date and we
> ended up going to that pizza place on the other side of the
> river. I can't remember what the name of it was now. It was
> the A-framed place beside of the Coast-to-Coast Motel. Any-

way, that day was such a nerve-racking day for me; I stayed in a state of panic and kept thinking I would just call him and cancel the date.

Well, of course my friends would not allow it. And he was so excited I couldn't bear to hurt his feelings.

That evening around 6:00 p.m. he picked me up and off we went to eat together for the first time. I was literally shaking and he, of course, was smiling from ear to ear. We pulled in and I said please let's just go riding or something and forget about eating. He turned off the car and sat there. No way was he budging. I had agreed to go and he was determined that this was the day to break the fear I had. He kept saying that after this we could sit together at the floral shop and eat each day. Again, he was so excited about that.

Well, we ordered a small pizza and two Cokes. Of course we ate in Rover, his jeep. No way was I going inside. He agreed to that. As long as we were sitting together eating that's all he wanted. He went in and ordered and brought the food out to Rover. We opened the box and took out a slice for each of us, and as he was closing the box it tipped and half the pizza went onto the floor. We laughed so hard we cried. Evidently, he was actually more nervous than I was. He went to pick up the pizza that dropped out and hit his Coke, which went onto the floor too. At this point we were cracking up. I was sitting there sticking pizza into my mouth and wasn't even thinking about my fear anymore. How could I be any messier than he had just been? Well, he ended up spilling his drink three times before it was over. He even had to go and order another one. It was the best experience ever and we just had the best time.

After that we always ate together. And believe it or not he always had a way of making me feel comfortable by spilling or dropping something on himself. It was one of the best evenings of my life that I will always remember!

Mecot would also bring her home for family dinners. He would take her fishing. He would spend time with her and her family. They were the sweetheart couple of Hinton High School and our small town.

Mecot's pet name for Tammy soon became "Rat." He decided to shorten her last name from Ratliff to Rat. Daddy was chuckling so much when Mecot first referred to Tammy as Rat. Especially when he had told Daddy that he was going to take Rat for some ice cream at Dairy Queen.

Mecot always made sure he was showered up, clean-shaven, and smelling like Musk (at the time his favorite cologne). He would spend more time in the bathroom than me and my older sister combined.

He drove a bright yellow Jeep Cherokee. Almost every day you could spot Mecot and Rat passing through town in "Rover." His love for Rover was a very close second to Rat. It was always clean and shiny.

Rat was a patient girlfriend from the start. She tolerated me tagging along with them quite a bit. She had every right to complain but she never did. I think she realized that Mecot and I shared a special bond. I, too, adored him as my big brother and she respected our relationship. We went to the movies, the mall, our two local restaurants (Dairy Queen and Pizza Hut) together.

She eventually became my best friend. When the three of us weren't together you could almost always find Rat and me cruising around in Rover while Mecot was busy at football practice or mowing neighbors' yards.

Believe it or not, the favorite pastime of teenagers in Hinton at that time was to cruise around town and end up either at Bellepoint Park or "The Pits." The Pits was the area where the boats would launch into Bluestone Lake during the Water Festival each year, but it also became a great hangout for teenagers too.

We'd park our cars facing the lake and crank up our radios, listening to bands like Supertramp, Blue Oyster Cult, and Lynyrd Skynyrd. Throwing back a few bottles of Boone's Farm Country Quenchers and Strawberry Hill enlightened our time together hanging out talking about the high school football games, school, who was dating whom....

It was also a great place at night to park and make out. I recall conversations with Tammy, minus the complete details, that led me to believe they liked to park and make out at The Pits quite often.

It is a beautiful spot—you can see the big metal arched bridge above and the water sparkling in the moonlight like diamonds, and if the windows were down you could hear the water gently lapping against the lake's edge.

It was a great place to bring your date for some sweet romance in an undisturbed, peaceful setting. It was the ideal place for true high school sweethearts like Mecot and Rat to get to know each other.

Onward to Concord College

M ECOT AND TAMMY KEPT THEIR ROMANCE alive all through high school. They attended all the dances, proms, football games, and so on…. When they graduated in May 1979, their romance was still going strong. They both decided to attend Concord College in Athens, West Virginia. Athens is another little town just up the mountain from Hinton. It is a little college town tucked away amid the mountaintop.

Mecot once again became well-known on this college campus. He was the freshman fellow students from other places were talking about. He walked on campus exuding a smile, charm, and friendliness and projected a strong drive for success. Tammy did not concern herself with the other freshmen girls that took a liking to Mecot. He was all about Tammy. She could walk with confidence on campus knowing her relationship with Mecot was one of complete devotion. All it took was for the two of them to be together on campus for other interested girls and charming fraternity boys to get the message that they were a couple for the long haul.

College was an exciting time for Mecot. His sense of camaraderie was always with him. He had no enemies and once he befriended you he was loyal forever, from childhood friends to high school friends and eventually on to college friends.

After Mecot saw all the hype about the fraternity rush, he decided he wanted to join a fraternity. What better way to live a life of brotherhood than among your own fraternity? So he decided to participate in the rush process his freshman year. There are only a handful of fraternities at Concord but he honed in on one that was pulling at his heartstrings. Every fraternity was throwing him bids. They all knew he would be such an asset and so fun to have as part of their brotherhood. He was well-thought-of by most all of them, but he ended up a Pi Kappa Alpha.

Mecot loved this fraternity and mentioned to me on occasion their fraternity saying. It goes like this:

> Pi Kappa Alpha's members strive to be
> Scholars, Leaders, Athletes, and Gentlemen,
> and they seek excellence in everything they do.

No wonder Mecot joined this fraternity. Those were ideals that he lived by daily.

Very often, he would come home from college with Rover loaded up with fraternity brothers. My family always had the door open and warm food to share with any of our friends growing up, and now Mecot's fraternity brothers were especially welcome. My mom just loved when she would see Rover pulling up the driveway with a jeep full of Mecot's bros.

Threase was already married at the time and living just down the hillside from our family home. Daddy bought her that house for her wedding gift because he did not want her moving too far away from home.

Threase married one of Mecot's best high school friends. His name was Ron. And whenever they saw Rover coming up the hill they would jump out their back door and walk up the hillside to hang out together. We would have a feast! Fresh fish and rice seemed to be a staple at the house, and we always had more than enough to feed Mecot's fraternity brothers. And believe me, his fraternity brothers loved Mom and Dad's home-cooked meals!

We all loved when he came home. My aunts would come from their downtown apartment, and Mecot's neighborhood and high school friends would come too. It was a party whenever he was home. My aunts would play the piano and guitar, his friends would play the banjo with him, and we would all sing and dance into the wee hours of the night. His fraternity brothers joined right in just like they were family, which they were to us. If Mecot loved them and respected them enough to become part of their brotherhood then we loved and respected them as family too!

College life was great for Mecot, or so it seemed. One of his high school buddies, Randy Bowles, remembers taking a philosophy class with him. One day, Mecot and the instructor got into a debate over what it meant to be an American.

At the time, Mecot was wearing a patriotic T-shirt that represented his devotion to our country. He stood highly confident wearing that T-shirt. The story goes that Mecot got up in front of the class and gave his own philosophy on what it meant to be an American.

Of course, this speech was made after the approval of the instructor. Mecot did ask with great respect if he could come before the class and share his philosophy. Needless to say, after he was done he graciously received a standing ovation from the rest of the class and a firm hand-shake and smile from the instructor. The professor declared that he could not have said it better than Mecot had said it himself.

Freshman year was over before we knew it. Mecot and Tammy were still going strong. However, Tammy had made the decision to transfer to Marshall University in Huntington, West Virginia, her sophomore year to pursue a nursing career. This was just the time that Mecot was pondering college life. His patriotism was stirring in his heart and he was thinking he could do more in this world serving our country as a U.S. Marine than by going down the college path.

It was the fall of 1980, and Tammy had left for Marshall University. Mecot had helped her load her belongings into her small car and kissed her good-bye. The end of freshman year at Concord became an eye-opener to both of them and their relationship together. They were still always connected, yet being in different colleges in two different towns, they decided to allow each other the opportunity to date other people.

Tammy settled in at Marshall. She was quickly making new friends and lived in a dormitory with fellow nursing majors. Her time was mainly spent in study groups; however, occasionally she would go out with the girls. She missed Mecot. Many handsome young men approached her but she was not ready to disconnect from Mecot.

Her communication with Mecot was through the dorm hallway phone that was shared by all the girls. When Mecot called, Tammy would run down the hallway with a huge grin on her face. They would talk for hours at a time, holding up the line from her friends on the same floor. But they were sweet and usually gave her the time with him. She had talked about him so much that her dorm mates had become smitten with their past relationship and all the fun, romantic times they shared together.

12

Rat Proposal

ON OCTOBER 28, 1980, MECOT WAS OFFICIALLY approved and enlisted in the United States Marine Corps.

He didn't wait a second to come barreling through our porch door with his formal paper. It was titled "Statement of Understanding of Military Obligations Assumed by Me upon My Enlistment in the Marine Corps or Marine Corps Reserve."

He had already signed it and was on his way to becoming a Marine.

After the shock of his decision, we rallied around Mecot in support of his new career path. That was his calling and we were all going to stand behind him one hundred percent. Our home was the new bustling hub of activity for the next few weeks.

Many of Daddy's patients would drop off homemade jams and jellies, cakes and pies, quilts and homemade knitted sweaters for Mecot. They wanted to make sure he had a great send-off. We were overwhelmed by such support. I am sure my parents had moments of worry but they never, ever showed it to me and my sister or the town, and most especially not to Mecot.

Mecot hovered around the house for the next few weeks and thanked everyone who came by to give him a hug and wish him luck. But one particular day he left the house and did not return that evening.

We did not have cell phones back then, so we just trusted that he was safe and merely needed some time away. Little did we know he went to the jeweler in Princeton and purchased a beautiful engagement ring, then drove to Marshall University in Huntington.

Tammy had no idea he was coming to visit, let alone that he was coming with the intention of asking her to marry him. Mecot did not want to leave for boot camp with the fear that someone else would whisk Tammy away from him.

He drove directly from Princeton to Huntington in Rover. He was singing songs the whole way, smiling ear to ear. Around and around the mountains he drove. He finally arrived on campus at Marshall.

She had told him during previous phone conversations which dorm she lived in. He parked, walked on campus, and started asking students where Holderby Hall was located.

He finally found Holderby, and then he proceeded to ask where Tammy's dorm room was located. Everyone was staring at him. He felt a little funny.

With great confidence and a heart full of love, he walked down her hallway and knocked on her door. He got down on one knee. By this point everyone was peeking their heads out of their rooms. Tammy opened the door, expecting to see someone at eye level. But when she looked down she just started crying the biggest tears ever.

Mecot was on one knee with the jewelry box already opened. Her smile was just as brilliant as the diamond ring that lay in the velvet-covered box. "Tammy, I love you more than anything in this world. Please marry me."

Tammy was crying so hard. She was speechless and having a hard time getting anything to come out her mouth. Her words were expressed through the stream of tears rolling down her cheeks. Eventually she uttered a soft-spoken yes. And Mecot placed the ring on her finger. Everyone in the dorm was clapping and crying.

It was starting to get late in the evening. Tammy really wanted Mecot to stay over so he would not have to drive late on the curvy roads to get home. However, he insisted on going home. He wanted to finish his fall semester out and he did not want to miss class the next day. He was one to stick to a commitment once he made it, and he was not going to quit his college classes. Even though he had already committed to the U.S. Marine Corps in January, he still wanted to finish out the semester.

The next evening the family was all sitting at the table and Mecot, out of nowhere, announced, "She said yes and we are getting married!" Oh my, that got the party started. We were all singing and dancing with the aunts all night long as we took turns shouting with glee to Tammy over the phone. She was planning on withdrawing from Marshall after that semester was done. She was going to come home to plan what felt like the biggest wedding in the history of Hinton. Mecot would be done with boot camp on April 3, 1981. And the wedding would take place one month later on May 9, 1981. He would come home to marry his high school sweetheart and then report back to Camp Lejuene. This made Mecot's good-bye not so sad, knowing that he would be home in a few months and we would be having a big, big wedding.

My alarm clock was buzzing like crazy at 5:30 a.m. on that frosty-cold morning of January 1981. I was not going to miss giving my brother a huge good-bye hug and receive his infamous big bear hug back! It was still dark, chilly, and quiet except for the continuous rolling sound of the flow of the river.

He left our home with his big smirky grin and said he would be seeing us real soon for the wedding. Daddy and Mom, of course, held it together for my sister and me. Although there was a quick moment when I looked over at Daddy and Mom and sensed fear and admiration for their son; he, in return, looked over at them with love, respect, and his infamous grin, mouthing the words, "I love you" and "Thank you, Mom and Dad."

He gave us all hugs. Mine was a biggie. He always lifted me off my feet and swung me around. The Mecot bear hug was the best! And then he placed me gently back down on the ground, looked me in the eye, and happily said, "Be good, little sister. You know I love you and I'll always be looking out for you no matter what!" He just had a way of making everything OK despite the fact that he was leaving for boot camp and we were all going to miss him terribly. But it was really cool and comforting knowing that he was going to be an all-American warrior. Something he always dreamed of doing. He was now on his way to living his dream. He saw me tearing up and winked at me and completely reassured me he was coming home soon.

We all stood together by the porch door and waved to him as Rover rolled down the driveway. It gave me comfort knowing that Mecot was leaving with the knowledge that his bride-to-be would be home planning their wedding and he was on his way to becoming a United States Marine. It was something he had instinctively wanted to do since playing with army men as a little boy growing up in the mountains. It was at that very moment when he drove down the driveway, waving and smiling out the window, that I knew Mecot was my American brother, soon to be an official American warrior of the United States Marine Corps.

13

Destination: Boot Camp

M ECOT HAD TO REPORT TO THE MARINE CORPS enlistment office in Princeton at 6:45a.m. for departure to Parris Island, South Carolina. Rover slowly backed down our frosty hillside driveway with Mecot smiling his smirky grin and waving the whole way down. All his windows were rolled down despite the cold air, and Lynyrd Skynyrd was cranked up on his cassette player. His head was stuck out the window like a happy doggie going on a joyride with its owner as he stared at the mountains and rivers that were his natural playground for years.

He was picking up one of his very best high school buddies named Ronnie (not to be confused to Ron, Threase's husband) to keep him company during the ride and drop him at the enlistment office in Princeton, West Virginia. Afterward, Ronnie was bringing Rover back home.

He tried to keep everything lighthearted. Ronnie remembers Mecot's conversation while driving. Mecot kept joking with him that it wasn't too late for him to enlist and hop on the bus. Mecot was willing to be that all-forever faithful friend and sneak him on board. Ronnie just laughed and graciously rejected the idea but let Mecot know he was his friend for life and he'd be in Hinton anxiously awaiting his return.

Up the mountain they drove, past the Bluestone Dam and Bluestone Lake where Mecot water-skied, fished, and camped every summer since he was five years old.

As they approached Athens, home of Concord College, he had no idea what was awaiting him. The curvy road wound around the mountaintop where the fraternities placed their Greek letters and banners. It was there that Mecot's fraternity brothers were standing, holding a huge banner that said, YOUR PI KAPPA ALPHA BROTHERS WANT YOU…TO KICK ASS IN THE MARINES, BROTHER MECOT!

Rover slowed down. Mecot rolled down the window and with a huge smile gave them all a salute. It was the first of many for him. After completing that salute, Mecot would have wondered if he'd even done it correctly. But he knew they'd be showing him in only a matter of hours. He rolled up the window and thought to himself about how much he loved his fraternity and all that brotherhood represented to him. He was getting even more pumped up at the idea of an even bigger brotherhood awaiting him. This brings to my mind an old saying: "Brothers do not always have to share the last name."

So Mecot pulled into the parking lot of the enlistment office, gave Rover one last pat, and gave Ronnie the keys. Once again, Mecot smiled that smirky grin and hugged Ronnie and affirmed, "I'll be back in a few months ready to go fishing together."

And he gazed at that bus a moment before he actually boarded. He took a deep breath, and without hesitation he took his first step aboard the bus and looked back at Rover. Mecot gave Ronnie a thumbs-up. Ronnie gave him a salute, and with that Mecot was on board and heading to basic training at Parris Island, South Carolina. He knew he was on his way to become a warrior. Something he always dreamed of becoming since he was a little boy playing with a bucket of soldiers.

It was a long seven-hour bus ride. That was a lot of time for Mecot to really think about his new adventure in life. He was energized about his decision; however, seeing his family trying to hold back tears was hard. He knew that we understood he had made the ultimate decision to sacrifice his life for our country, and he knew he had our most utmost respect, support, and love. Later he wrote in one of his first letters home that his mind kept going back to the good-bye hugs and that he knew he was greatly loved by all of us and the entire town of Hinton. And that reassured him of his decision and helped get him through the rigorous boot-camp training. He knew those same big hugs would be waiting on him when he got back home.

Mecot noticed the shadow of the mountains seemed to be getting smaller and smaller as the bus drove farther down east to South Carolina. His silence and introspection of his life, mixed with his nervous excitement about the future, was soon overcome by his outgoing personality and ability to make friends wherever he went.

He decided that he had spent enough time thinking about his personal journey and expectations of boot camp, and so he struck up conversation with his fellow recruits. There were only a few on the bus but they shared stories of their families back home. Mecot often wondered what made them decide to join the Marines. He never asked. He already respected where they came from and he enjoyed hearing their stories of family life back home. And he knew in a matter of hours they would all be on the same team and in the same boat, so to speak. I think for him, he knew that it was a calling to serve our country and he could already feel the camaraderie with his fellow recruits who felt the exact same way. They were now bonded in a way that only a few can understand. These young men were willingly giving of themselves, by their own free will, to do something more extraordinary than ever imagined. They were soon to be American brothers, each one coming from a family, a neighborhood, a church, a town that supplied their decision-making, soon molding them into modern day warriors serving our country in the United State Marine Corp.

And so the bus arrived. Off came the recruits. Some were wearing their high school football jackets, some jeans and dress shirts; some had long hair, some short hair; and they were African American, Filipino, Caucasian, and Hispanic. They all exited the bus with the same look: a look of nervousness and excitement with a little bit of fear thrown in. It's that fear of the unknown, and they were probably thinking, *What did I get myself into?* But knowing in their hearts they made a great decision.

Each step from the bus brought them closer to the most historic signage for the U.S. Marine Corps: THROUGH THESE PORTALS PASS PROSPECTS FOR THE WORLD'S FINEST FIGHTING FORCE: UNITED STATES MARINES.

As stated on the Marines.com website, "Honor, courage, and commitment form the bedrock of every Marine's character, and guide every decision they will make all around the world. Under demanding conditions, these are the values Marines count on, so that their nation can count on them."[9] I knew that Mecot's character completely fit this mold. He was a natural at honor, courage, and commitment. Growing up with an American brother who always put others first, who always found courage to get through frightening times and who, once he was your friend, was committed to you for life, inspired me every day to become just like him. If Mecot made a commitment he would never break it. You could always count on him.

So he slowly exited the Greyhound bus, walked to the portal, and smiled when he looked up and read the sign. He actually felt comforted knowing that he made the decision to become a U.S. Marine: the few, the proud.

It was a whole different world. In the first few hours Mecot's thick black hair was shaved down to his scalp. It went from medium length to no length to something like a very trimmed-up Chia Pet.

The mood was extremely quiet. He and his new comrades learned quickly to speak only when spoken to and to follow all orders.

The following article by Amber J. Cabrera provides a peek into Marine Corps boot camp. Cabrera is a Marine Corps veteran and writer.

---

[9] "Recruit Training," Marines.com, accessed May 12, 2013, http://www.marines.com/becoming-a-marine/recruit-training.

Processing (which can also be referred to as "receiving") is the first step prior to entering Marine Corps boot camp. You will most likely either arrive to Parris Island late at night or early morning. The darkness of these times is used to disorient you on purpose. From the second you get off of the bus and onto the yellow footprints, you will be an individual no more. Processing is the period of time (about 2–5 days) that you will have everything you need for the next 13 weeks issued to you, your paperwork signed, medical exams completed, and your world turned upside down.

Marine Corps boot camp is 12 weeks of training plus one week of processing. During this time several things are going to happen to you.

1. Before you either get off of the bus or get into the building, the receiving drill instructors are going to educate you about three laws of the Uniform Code of Military Justice (UCMJ). Roughly, these are Article 86 (Absence without Leave), Article 91(Disobedience to a Lawful Order) and Article 93 (Disrespect to a Senior Officer). None of these are up for negotiation and all must be followed for the entire time you are enlisted in the Marine Corps.

2. The drill instructors will inform you that the only proper way to address them will be "Sir" or "Ma'am."

3. Within the first day and a half you will not be able to sleep but will be expected to function coherently. For the males, you will have your hair shaved off. Every piece of civilian clothing and possession you bring will be turned over and stored in a warehouse until graduation. If I were you (and I once was), only take what your recruiter told you to bring, if anything. Don't buy a lot of things you think you will need because they will just make you throw them away. The Marine Corps doesn't play.

4. Everything that you will need during your time in boot camp will be issued to you, including uniforms, toiletries, field gear, and your rifle. However, they are not doing this out of the goodness of their heart; your pay will be deducted the expense of all of these items.

5. You will be taught the basics of marching, drilling, how to wear your uniforms, how to eat, drink, shower, and even how to go to the bathroom. No, I am not kidding.

6. The Initial Strength Test (IST) will be conducted and you must pass this or you will be retained and put into the Physical Conditioning Platoon (PCP) where you will not be able to start your training until you can pass the IST. You do NOT want to get put here, so I would advise you to start running and training BEFORE you go to boot camp.

Finally, you will be taken to your barracks to meet your Senior Drill Instructor and his or her assistants. THIS is where the real fun begins!

The processing portion of Marine Corps boot camp is designed to get you prepared to start your training. It also shakes you into a surreal reality where you start asking yourself, "What did I get myself into?" Just follow the instructions given to you and do exactly what they tell you to do and you will be fine.[10]

I could not wait to hear all about his boot camp adventure. Mecot would send me letters all the time. I immediately ripped them open in our small-town post office. I could never wait to get back to my home to read his letters.

---

[10] Amber J. Cabrera, "Marine Corps Boot Camp Review: Processing," Yahoo! Voices, April 4, 2011, http://voices.yahoo.com/marine-corps-boot-camp-review-processing-8189011.html?cat=31.

The postmaster was one of our neighbors, named Mr. Graham, Keith Graham's father. He would always peek out to the front area when he heard me laughing. He would just smile and express, "Oh, another letter from that brother of yours, eh?" Everyone knew it must be from Mecot. Not only did I talk about him all the time but also the entire town knew he was at boot camp, and they all had inquiring minds. I always shared what was written in the letters right down to the details of what he was doing in basic training. He could still grab everyone's attention even if miles away in a field doing assault drills.

I wrote to him as much as possible. I thought it would be so sad to be a recruit and not receive any mail on mail day. So I was sending letters to Mecot pretty regularly, and so were my mom and sister. Tammy was sending double the number, for sure.

One area of training that Mecot found a bit comfortable was the rifle range. Mecot was familiar with rifles, as he had grown up hunting for deer every fall. Although Mecot never came home with a deer after hunting, he always had some great stories of how the deer ran off or he just missed it. But we think he just did not have the heart to shoot a deer, even though he definitely knew how to use a rifle!

I think he just enjoyed going up to the hunting camp and hanging out with his friends, playing the banjo in the evenings, singing songs, chewing his Beech-Nut tobacco, and throwing back a few Miller Lites! We would often go to our farm on the weekends and shoot at targets and empty milk jugs for fun. He had great target skills.

And yes, he learned the Rifleman's Creed, as expected of all recruits. His way of memorizing it was writing it down on paper, so in one of his letters he actually wrote out the creed to me, word for word. When I saw the envelope I thought it was a big letter with lots of exciting stuff that he was going to tell me. It was actually the creed. He wrote that it would be a good idea for me to know this stuff too—with a "Ha" written at the end. I was very impressed that he wrote it from memory:

This is my rifle.

There are many like it, but this one is mine. It is my life. I must master it as I must master my life.

Without me my rifle is useless. Without my rifle, I am useless. I must fire my rifle true. I must shoot straighter than the enemy who is trying to kill me. I must shoot him before he shoots me. I will....

My rifle and I know that what counts in war is not the rounds we fire, the noise of our burst, or the smoke we make. We know that it is the hits that count. We will hit....

My rifle is human, even as I am human, because it is my life. Thus, I will learn it as a brother. I will learn its weaknesses, its strengths, its parts, its accessories, its sights and its barrel. I will keep my rifle clean and ready, even as I am clean and ready. We will become part of each other.

Before God I swear this creed. My rifle and I are the defenders of my country. We are the masters of our enemy. We are the saviors of my life....

So be it, until victory is America's and there is no enemy.

—*Major General William H. Rupertus, "Rifleman's Creed"*

Mecot was really showing his leadership skills. He was, as usual, helpful to his fellow recruits while jamming through all the physical exercises from obstacle course to pugil stick. He would write letters and tell me how he was always the one left standing and he loved it! He said rappelling was difficult. He did suffer a slight nervousness with heights but he eventually overcame that too! As his training was getting closer to the end, he talked about the amphibious drills and the helicopter basics and about successfully learning how to implement camouflage and concealment techniques.

But his letters always ended with something he was missing from home. He definitely missed Mom's fried chicken. I would hear that quiet often in his letters too! He could not wait to have my aunts' Filipino food. He also knew I loved to bake cookies and cakes. He conveyed he was ready for his welcome-home chocolate cake, fresh from the oven and made especially by his li'l sis with lots of love.

The letters kept coming. He would talk about the gas chamber training and how weird he felt being exposed to that stuff and how he really focused on the instructor for that training segment.

In his last few letters from basic training, he just mentioned how excited he was about seeing all of us for his graduation. He was so completely pumped up on being a Marine. He really jammed through the confidence course and the assault course and it was on to final inspection. Wow! He recalled putting his complete uniform on and feeling like he was ready to tackle the world. He was just days away from graduation for the United States Marine Corps. He was in the homestretch. I was counting down the days too!

14

Official U.S. Marine

APRIL 3, 1981 WAS A BEAUTIFUL SUNNY DAY. I had ridden with Mom and Dad in our little VW Dasher from Hinton the day before. We had planned to meet Tammy and her family at the hotel. When we got there, Tammy and I just got so giddy with excitement! We were like a couple of little girls! We were just a few hours away from seeing Mecot and witnessing his graduation in the United States Marines. We could not have been more stirred up!

I had gone shopping for the perfect dress the weekend before. It had pastel flowers all over and little sparkly beads. I was hoping he would spot me.

So away we drove from the hotel onto the base. I had never been on a military base before. I was so fascinated. Everything was perfect.

The guards respectfully directed us. We parked and meandered up the crowded stadium seating. Lots of other families were all gathered around the field where the ceremonies were being held.

I could see the love and admiration in each of their faces. What a huge accomplishment and blessing we all felt that day for our American brothers!

My brother was selected to be in the color guard. I could not wait for the ceremonies to begin. And when they did, I anxiously gazed at each of the color guardsmen until I could affix my eyes onto Mecot. He was on the end carrying his rifle upon his broad shoulder and looking very

dignified as he marched with pride and confidence. My big brother was
all grown up and a real American warrior. Just as he wanted it. My big
brother: a United States Marine.

All I could think about was how we all came to be there that day. It
was Mecot's decision that he made on his own free will and a decision
that made him very, very happy. We were all there that day thanks to
Mecot and his lifelong dream to become a warrior.

I looked at him marching on that field and it compelled me to reflect
on the days of him playing along the river with his toy soldiers and his
neighborhood friends—from those days until this one, now I was staring
onto the military field and seeing my big brother as a real warrior in the

Mecot's graduation from boot camp at Parris Island, South
Carolina. He is on the far left, marching next to the Marine
carrying the American flag.

real United States Marine Corps. I was just happy and blessed to share with all the other families I was sitting with that day. I pointed in admiration and said, "Hey, there he is. That is my big brother. He's the one in the color guard getting ready to march past us. He's on the end with the rifle." He was looking forward but I did notice what appeared to be a wink and a little bit of that smirky grin. It wasn't too big of a smirk but enough to make it known that he was happy to have all of us there. He spotted us and I was so thrilled!

After the ceremonies, all the cadets were reuniting with their families. I could not find Mecot anywhere. We were in a swarm of sharp-dressed, well-mannered new Marines all searching for their families. From a distance they all looked alike, walked alike, and even talked alike; however, there was one big, slightly intimidating Marine marching toward us. I did not recognize the well-built, highly confident Marine at first... until I saw that smirky grin that could belong to no other than my American brother.

Then he took off his head cover and it became clear that it was Mecot, and he picked up his pace when he saw Tammy and the rest of us. Tammy picked up her pace too! They ran to each other as soon as their eyes connected. It was one of the sweetest hugs I have ever witnessed. It was like something out of the movies. He completely embraced her tall, thin body, lifted her off her feet, and spun her, with her flowered dress circling around the both of them. After the spin came the long kiss. His big hands were gently caressing her sweet, rosy cheeks and her soft, tiny hands were firmly holding on to his chiseled face. They just did not want to let go of each other.

All I could do was smile the biggest smile ever. He looked great and they just made the cutest couple ever. My smile turned into a smile plus happy tears. The tears just kept rolling down my little browned-skinned cheeks.

As he walked toward me he was also asking me what I thought about all this commotion. I was speechless and standing motionless in awe

Mecot in his dress blues—officialy a U.S. Marine.

that he was an American warrior: my big brother—an official United States Marine.

He picked me up off my feet and gave me a big hug. "I did it, little sister! What do ya think?" I was still absolutely speechless. He chuckled. "Elisa, you are never shy for words. Now this is a historic moment. My little sister is at a loss for words." And he chuckled even more. After my feet came back down to earth, I had him bend down, and I whispered in his ear, "You just keep amazing me, and I believe I am the luckiest little sister in the whole wide world!" He smiled. "That's the little sister I know and love. I knew you couldn't be quiet for too long, and I was right! Some things do not change, huh?"

The hugs just did not stop. Mom and Dad waited patiently for theirs. And Tammy's family waited patiently for theirs too! We all gathered around him with nothing but love and admiration that day. It was a great day for all of us!

As we were walking to our cars with Mecot, he wanted to introduce us to a few of his fellow Marines. However, he was always quick to advise them, "Now, don't be getting any ideas about my pretty little sister. I'll take you down and do you some serious harm." He looked at me and said, "I'll always protect you, Elisa, even if it's from my fellow jarheads that think you're cute. We all know you are adorable. It's genetic. But you are my little sister first and foremost." He looked back and winked at them. "See ya, guys." I looked back, shrugged my shoulders, and said, "He is my big brother, ya know!" I smiled a little flirty grin and strolled off as they strutted away too.

That night, back at the hotel, as I lay in bed reflecting upon this most amazing day, I thought to myself about how my brother, sister, and I grew up in a small American town with a rich heritage of American military families. We were raised by a Filipino father who valued our freedoms and conveyed that message every day. Our mom, dad, and small town had really instilled in all of us, especially Mecot, those core values that created the Marine in him.

The next day we all checked out of the little hotel that accommodated almost all the recruits' family members for that very important graduation day. Mecot helped load our little VW Dasher with all our luggage. It was like a small station wagon; however, it was capable of holding many pieces of luggage. You would think Tammy and I had packed for a three-week stay in the Arctic.

He was now strong, muscular, and well-groomed, with a nice flat-top haircut. He had a white tank top that totally made obvious his huge biceps and chest. According to Tammy, his brown skin against the white tank top was quiet attractive. She whispered to me, "Check out my man. And just how adorable is he?"

He walked with great confidence and humility; however, the one thing that did not change was his smirky grin. It was big as ever that day. He was with his bride-to-be, her family, and our family, and—just as special—he was on his way home to the mountains to be surrounded by all his friends.

15

Wedding Bliss

T AMMY HAD DRIVEN MECOT'S SECOND LOVE of his life, Rover, all the way from West Virginia to his graduation in South Carolina. Oh how Mecot's eyes lit up when he gazed upon his big, bright yellow jeep in the hotel parking lot! Rover came packed with lots of memories: pulling friends out of ditches with the winch; taking me to cheerleading camp, loaded with the entire cheerleading squad cheering the whole way; taking trips to Kentucky to visit our great-uncle and great-aunt; transporting us and our friends to prom; and driving Dad to the hospital for emergencies when everyone else was snowed in.

So after all of the luggage that could fit in the VW Dasher was loaded, he began to load Rover with the rest of it and all of his belongings from boot camp. Mecot strolled over to the passenger door and opened it. Then, winking at Tammy, he softly said, "Get in, Rat. It's time to go home and get married." Mom, Dad, and I loaded into the VW Dasher. Tammy's parents and her cousin crammed into their Dodge Dart, and we followed Rover back to Hinton.

It was a long drive but it went by quickly. Mom and Dad and I chatted about the graduation and how all the pomp and circumstance amazed each of us. We knew that Mecot was a part of something big, something extraordinary, and was part of a loyal, ever-lasting brotherhood.

And we knew that he was right where he felt he belonged. He was part of the U.S. Marine Corps and he sure showed it in every way imaginable. He loved the Corps! And he was ready to go home and let his hometown family of Hinton know how happy he was with his decision to become a Marine.

As we left the base, I gazed out the window at the new recruits marching in cadence and the view of the barracks and life in general on a military base. It was so foreign to me, yet I could see in the recruits' eyes that each one of them was special just like Mecot.

After that thought, I realized this military base and these recruits no longer seemed foreign but familiar to me. Just as familiar as my brother as each one of them will march and run; each one will learn and train to be a U.S. Marine.

After that reassuring and peaceful thought, I looked in front of us at Rover, with Mecot driving and Tammy in the passenger seat. I could see the entire profile of Tammy's face as she moved her lips nonstop except to occasionally kiss him on the cheek. I am sure she was giving him the total schedule of events hour by hour up until the start of their romantic mountain wedding. I could see Mecot's head nod in affirmation more than once. Last glance, he put his arm around her and gave her a big squeeze.

Looking out the side window, I noticed the signs for the East River Mountain Tunnel. I learned at a young age from our family travels that when we saw signs for the tunnel we were getting very close to home. Soon we were close enough to read the sign: Turn on Your Headlights.

It is 5,412 feet long and crosses the state lines of Virginia and West Virginia, and that day it was dark and dripping with moisture. You could hear the loud echoes of the car motors as they passed by you.

I often wondered how long it must have taken to carve such an enormous hole out of the gigantic mountain. I am always amazed each time I went through it. Even to this day. Talk about teamwork and brotherhood. I'm pretty sure those elements were key in blowing through a mountain and building a tunnel.

So once on the other side I could see the large Welcome to West Virginia sign. It was at that point we could not stop talking about the wedding.

We were minutes from home and there was so much to be done! The wedding invitations had been sent out and on May 9, 1981, the good people of Hinton would share in Mecot and Tammy's blessed wedding day.

We only had a few weeks to create a wedding of a lifetime for my American brother and his bride. He had been given his orders to report to Camp Lejeune, North Carolina, in three weeks.

It was a fantastic homecoming. Rover slowed down as we got close to home and we were driving across the Bluestone Lake Bridge. Mecot was slowing down to take in his old stomping ground mile by mile. We drove down the mountain, past the large lake that he fished and swam in. In my mind, I could still see his big blue tent along the banks, where he practically lived during the summer months.

The water was shimmering like a million diamonds on that sunny afternoon. You could hear the boats on the water and see the curves of the mountains that had been carved out by the gently rolling waves over time.

The road into Hinton wrapped around the mountains and looked over the lake. Many times after a winter storm when the snow would melt on the mountains, it was not uncommon to drive right upon fallen boulders in the middle of the road.

These were not little pebbles but large boulders. I was always amazed that the boulders never fell on cars as they were driving by. Believe it or not, all my life growing up there I never heard of anyone that was hurt from the falling rocks.

And whenever Mecot heard of a boulder falling, he would take me to see the road crew break up the boulders and shove them in the ditch. He always tried to lend a hand with Rover's winch but it just was not strong enough for these enormous stones. So we both would sit and watch in amazement at the size of these rocks and the effort it took for road crews to break them up and move them.

Still driving along the mountainside, we passed the Summers County Dam and followed Rover the last few miles down to the valley of Hinton, where the rivers and the roads converge. From that three-way stop we all went to the right. And we drove across the bridge and onto Green-brier Drive. Greenbrier Drive is the road adjacent to the Greenbrier River and the road to our driveway up the hillside to house number 1008.

This street holds many memories from the "John Boat, Jerry, and the Great Flood" adventure to ice hockey on the ponds and tubing down the river. It was great to be coming home to these fabulous memories with my big brother and knowing that he was now officially a Marine.

I couldn't wait to create more fun memories with him and Tammy, as the wedding was just a few days away! Rover's blinker was blinking to the right. And right up our driveway we were just about home. I could not help but hit the horn a dozen times while Daddy was driving. This was before cell phones, so the horn blowing was my way of telling everyone that Mecot was seconds away!

We pulled up the driveway and immediately you could see the huge rho-dodendrons along the hillside to the right. They were covered with vibrant hues of pinks and purples overflowing onto the driveway. On the left was the apple orchard with a combination of pure white blossoms and small bright green granny smith apples. Daddy must have planted at least ten to twelve trees crammed into the smallest area at the base of our driveway.

Those trees had lots of good and bad memories. Mecot, Threase, and I picked many an apple from Daddy's orchard. We would pick a few, eat a few, pick a few, eat a few. At any given time of day, one of us was pulling down an apple and biting into it right then and there underneath the shade of the widespread branches.

When the trees began to droop with apples and quite a few were on the ground, we would go and fill up buckets and bring them to Nanny. She would make homemade apple butter, and it was so yummy. She made it with a smooth consistency like peanut butter with a little bit of a bite due to the tartness of the granny smith apples. Once a spoonful was on your taste buds you knew you could not resist but eat the whole jarful.

But there were also the scary memories of Nanny marching to that or-chard and pulling off a nice firm branch that transformed instantly into what she called a "switch." Whenever we acted out of line she would bring out the switch and our bottoms would get a few good swats. She had zero tolerance for "bad mouthin" (meaning disrespect to her) and for not cleaning our rooms. We learned what respect meant at a very young age thanks to her diligence in raising us in our parent's absence while they worked in Daddy's office.

So past the orchard and up the hill Mecot was home! Outside our house stood our aunts, my sister and her husband, Mecot's best friend Jerry, and all our close neighbors. I was amazed after the horn blowing and the hugging how more and more neighbors and friends started showing up.

His homecoming eventually turned into a hometown gathering of banjo playing, singing, drinking, and dancing through the night. It ended up with the men on the porch listening to Mecot talk about his boot camp stories and the women at the kitchen table cutting netting. This was netting that my aunts had brought to make the rice bags to toss at Mecot and Tammy when they left for their honeymoon. We had ladies cutting the netting, ladies cutting the ribbons, ladies spooning out the rice, ladies putting it all together. It was like the most efficient assembly line I had ever witnessed. That night lasted into the early morning until the women ran out of rice. We must have made five hundred bags that night.

We were wrapping rice bags in rhythm with the banjo playing and we were laughing at how the singing seemed to get more and more boisterous as the night progressed.

Tammy was all smiles the entire time. Mecot would occasionally come in and check on her and the ladies. He would gently kiss her on the cheek. Once he looked up and smiled and said, "Ladies, this is my beautiful bride—wow!" He walked back again to be with the men and he looked back and said, "Wow!" Tammy turned three shades of red and could not stop smiling. I thought to myself, *If this is what real love is like, I cannot wait until my time.* I often dreamed of a forever romance with my high school sweetheart, just like Mecot and Tammy; I pondered if I was to be so lucky and in love like them one day. It was nothing but happiness and fun for the next few days. It seemed a great start to a long, happy life together.

The days passed quickly and before we knew it, it was May 9, 1981. It was an absolutely gorgeous spring day. I awoke to the sound of the early-morning train that went by from across the river. I looked out the kitchen window that overlooked our Oriental gardens and Daddy was already walking the gardens with the florist, our close friend, Sandy Pivont, and her staff. Daddy made sure the garden was perfectly manicured and ready to be embellished by wedding bells, lace, and an abundance of flowers, greenery, and ribbons.

Daddy's Oriental garden was well-known throughout West Virginia. Of course, we always hosted the West Virginia Water Festival Princess Luncheon, and we received visits from Senator Byrd and other politicians. His garden had been the front-page story of many West Virginia newspapers over the years.

What an achievement for my dad to turn a mountainside in West Virginia into a lavish Oriental garden with Filipino flare. He had imported statues from Italy and designed a special waterfall with the Lady of Lourdes at the forefront of the grotto. The clear, crisp water flowed down into two more ponds before it recirculated into the largest pond. This pond had imported Kai fish that swam about all spring and summer long. In the winters, the pond would freeze but once the ice melted, the fish would come to life again and begin flipping and flapping about.

Today, this spring day, the fish were gleefully flapping around almost as if they knew a huge celebration was going to take place in a matter of hours.

Daddy had imported from Italy four statutes of women that he placed in the garden. Each one was to represent the four ladies in his life: our mother, his mother, my sister, and me. He had also created a heart-shaped red rose garden for my mother.

On this day, the roses were blooming and you could smell the red rose aroma as soon as you walked down into the plaza; the rhododendrons were blooming and the grass could not be a more vibrant hue of green.

It really anchored all the bright colors of the flowers and roses surrounding the gardens.

The florist was creating a masterpiece with the garden bridge. She had placed a lovely wedding bell in the center and wrapped the railings in green ivy. The green ivy in contrast to the richly painted deep red bridge looked surreal.

Add a backdrop of dogwood trees with pink and white blossoms, a mountainside lush with foliage, and a hand-carved stone wall surrounding the pond and a gorgeous outdoor wedding reception site is created. Daddy wanted nothing more than perfection for his only son's wedding day. Today, May 9, 1981, God blessed him with the perfect sunny day with blue skies and crisp mountain air. His hard work creating an Oriental garden on a mountainside in West Virginia would soon become the place of magical wedding memories for Mecot and Tammy.

That morning Tammy was somewhat frantic that Mecot's tuxedo had not arrived yet. It was supposed to be in a week earlier, but there had been a shipping delay. Thankfully it did arrive; however, not until late in the morning. And there was a little problem. In Mecot's case the problem was literally "little." His tuxedo pants were two sizes too small.

When Mom came in to tell Tammy, you could have heard a pin drop. Mom whispered in her ear, "Do not worry; the tuxedo made it but it is two sizes too small in the pants. Mecot can squeeze into them but it's going to appear a little tight in the breeches. He is not able to button the jacket, but he's laughing his way into it as we speak." It was very quiet for what seemed an eternity. We did not know what she was thinking at that very moment or how she was going to react.

After the silence passed, Tammy started to laugh…and laugh…and laugh, and we all laughed with her. I wiped the sweat from my brow and laughed so hard my ab muscles started to hurt! It was then that I could really appreciate the reason Mecot loved her so.

Things started to move quickly and before we knew it we were at the church. Our little catholic church, the only Catholic church in Hinton, and it is the most beautiful of all the local churches if you don't mind me saying. It was on Main Street downtown. The tract of land it was built on was owned by the C&O railroad, and in 1878 Father D. P. Walsh paid one hundred dollars for the land and erected a one-story frame house of worship. This building is now the parochial house, and a "modern" brick church was later built in 1880 with a basement and is attached to the present-day parochial house.

In the basement is where Tammy and her bridesmaids made their final preparations. Tammy asked me to be a bridesmaid too! I was so excited that we were going to be family. Having her as a sis-in-law made me so excited, and Mecot knew I was thrilled for him.

One evening while at home it was just me and him sitting out on the porch and we were talking, and I told him, "Ya did good." He responded, "What are ya talking about, little Wauhatchie?" I replied, "You picked a great wife. I just love Tammy and I love hanging out with her." He chuckled with that big smirky grin and said, "Guess what? I love her and I like hanging out with her too!"

Well, back at the old church basement, little did Tammy know I was having a fashion crisis of my own too! I discovered my bridesmaid dress was much too long. I did not think to try it on earlier.

My mom said not to panic. She immediately took me to Murphy's Mart (like Wal-Mart) and found me the highest platform sandals she could find. We got back to the church and I put them on with the dress and it was perfect. The bigger problem was learning to walk in platform sandals. I practiced walking over and over again. Everyone in the family was laughing. My older sister was trying to show me. She was much more graceful than me. I'm better in a pair of Dr. Scholl's low-heel clogs. I definitely was not named "Grace" for a reason. I could hardly walk in those things. I felt taller than anyone, although I was the shortest bridesmaid she had chosen.

As I was touching up my makeup, Tammy emerged from one of the religious education classrooms that served as her dressing area. She looked radiant. Her smile was as astounding as her beautiful dress. As the florist was placing her veil upon her head, I could not help but tear up with the rest of her bridesmaids. This would be one of my brother's most important, special, and memorable occasions. He was marrying his gorgeous high school sweetheart.

He had grown up in this small all-American town. He had successfully completed boot camp and was an official U.S. Marine. That saying "It takes a village to raise a child" is so true. Mecot grew up as all-American as apple pie.

This town inspired and created the man Tammy was getting ready to marry. He had willing given his service to our country, with much inspiration coming from the good people of Hinton—the rich history of military families, the eternal bonding of his friends, and a father from the Philippines proud of his U.S. citizenship and a mother whose entire family served in the military. This was my American brother and soon-to-be husband to his stunning high school sweetheart.

It was time for the ceremony to start. We could hear the organ playing the processional from upstairs. We all lined up along the steps to the church entrance. As each of us would near the top of the stairs and stand at the doorway to the church, we could all hear and feel the vibration of the big church bell swinging back and forth and chiming as we each paused there until the signal was given to walk down the aisle.

I began walking up the hand-placed sandstone steps. I was holding on to the black iron railing for dear life. I had to learn quickly how to walk in high heels. I made it to the top and I took a moment to reflect on the church and all my memories of it. All three of us would come here every weekend with Mom and Dad for Mass, we had our First Communion here and our Christmas midnight Masses here, and both my aunts were married here. We witnessed Dad's significant contributions for renovations to the altar here. Daddy always wanted to help the church in every way imaginable. He instilled in us the importance of our church family and volunteering to preserve the rich history of the church. Today was another memory being added to the Camara family history here at St. Patrick's Catholic Church, Hinton, West Virginia.

When it was my turn to walk down the aisle, I was in awe. Every pew was full and there were even people standing in the back of the church. Yet, despite the hot afternoon sun coming through the stain-glass windows, everyone was all smiles. Our church was not air-conditioned at the time and all the ladies were fanning themselves with wedding programs. With the heat you would think people would be upset, but not today. Everyone was full of love, happiness, and support for Mecot and his bride.

So as I walked down the aisle, Mecot was there at the end standing with the priest. He had the biggest smile of all. I walked, careful not to trip in those platform sandals, toward him and then turned to the left of the altar with the other bridesmaids. Before I made my slow, steady turn, he looked over at me and winked. I just gave him a big smile back and nodded.

Next to walk down the aisle was Tammy's cousin. She was the maid of honor and the last to come in before Tammy. She gave Tammy a sweet kiss on the cheek before she began. She was already crying happy tears before she reached the end of the aisle. Luckily, she had tissues underneath her bouquet. She made it past Mecot and the priest with one little tear gently rolling down her cheek. Mecot nodded and said, "It's OK."

The official wedding march became louder. You could feel the organ pipes bellowing the traditional march as everyone began to stand up. Tammy looked absolutely stunning. She wore a beautiful full-length wedding gown with sheer sleeves and embroidered lace throughout. And her lace-embroidered veil cascaded to her small waistline. It was at her tiny waistline that she carried her bouquet of beautiful white roses, lavishly placed between the greenery and ribbon.

She was only steps away from her new life with Mecot. He was her knight in shining armor waiting for her at the end of the aisle. He could not take his eyes off her for one second. He was totally mesmerized by her beauty and sweetness. She began to gently glide toward him. She was starting to tear up and he was too! I do not believe there was a dry eye in the entire church.

It was a beautiful, traditional Catholic wedding ceremony.

After the most heartfelt wedding vows were exchanged and they had exchanged wedding rings, one of Daddy's office ladies, who also was a singer, sang the theme from the movie Ice Castles. She was singing as Mecot gently reached for Tammy's hand to help her up the altar to the unity candelabra.

The afternoon sun was slowing sinking into the mountains and the light passing through the stain-glass windows almost appeared to be glowing beautiful hues of amber directly onto the beautiful wedded couple as they were lighting the unity candle.

Once they lit the unity candle, they came down the altar for the end of the ceremony. The priest gave them their final blessing and with much elation proclaimed, "Mecot, you may now kiss your bride!" Mecot gently grasped Tammy's face with both hands, leaned toward her, and gently pressed his lips to hers. It was not just a little kiss. It was passionate, longer than the usual wedding kiss, and it had everyone once again in tears.

After the kiss, the priest announced, "I now present to you Mr. and Mrs. Mecot Camara." The organ pipes cranked up as they strolled out together arm in arm, beaming with smiles. After they walked out of the church, the bridesmaids and ushers gleefully proceeded down the aisle too! We were all anxious to give hugs to the newly married couple. And we were ready for the reception to begin.

After the traditional wedding photos were taken, Dad and Mom snuck out of church to make sure the house and gardens were ready for the wedding guests' arrival, and that the food and drinks were ready to be served too!

The wedding party was done with photos and ready to get to our house. As we approached Greenbrier Drive, there were cars parked on both sides of the road. Families were still parking and walking to the big event of Hinton.

Mecot and Tammy posing on our home's Oriental
bridge for their wedding picture.

Daddy had the classical music playing outdoors through the speakers,
the waterfall was coming down full force from the grotto, and soft-white
tissue wedding bells were dangling from every tree in the garden.

It was a fabulous reception. Set up everywhere were tables covered in
white linen and lace. There was an abundance of tapas, and champagne
fountains were flowing too. The sun was beginning to set as the sky
turned so many colors of soft yellow, orange, and deep purple.

It was the perfect time for the photographer to take more pictures of the happy couple with Mother Nature as the backdrop.

I had to chuckle for a moment when I saw the photographer taking a picture of Mecot and Tammy on the beautifully decorated garden bridge. Tammy had her arms wrapped around his left arm and Mecot had his large hands placed in front of his tuxedo breeches. I think he was trying to inconspicuously cover the tight tuxedo pants that were having a hard time staying buttoned.

So the sun eventually sank behind the mountaintop, and then Daddy flipped the switch on the night-lights. Tammy and Mecot just did not want the night to end.

As the evening progressed, Mecot and Tammy decided it was time to cut their wedding cake. Everyone came together by the heart-shaped rose garden. The wedding cake table was the centerpiece. The cake was three tiers high and stood on the linen and lace table with greenery adorned all around it. Not only was everyone talking about how beautiful it looked but also how aromatic it smelled. It had little white rose decorations all around it and the smell of the vanilla frosting overtook anyone walking by.

Tammy daintily placed a small piece in Mecot's mouth and Mecot, not nearly as careful as Tammy, drove a piece into her small mouth and placed a little drop of icing on her nose. It was too cute!

While everyone was eating their cake, Mecot and Tammy slipped away to change into their going-away attire.

My aunts made sure all the guests had at least two of the ornately decorated rice bags that we all had stayed up to make. Mecot and Tammy gleefully strolled from our front door down the steps to the driveway, which was lined on both sides with guests ready to launch the rice bags.

Tradition has it that the tossing of rice is a custom that is intended to give newlyweds good luck, and most of the items thrown at the couple represent fertility and abundance. Food has always been a popular choice because it symbolizes plentiful crops. Grains such as wheat and

Mecot and me at his wedding in front of our home's grotto
waterfall. I was laughing because he was making a funny
comment, under his breath, about his tight fitting pants.

rice were thrown over newlyweds in the hope that the couple would be
prosperous and have many children to work the land. The hope for this
blessing would turn into reality for my brother and his bride sooner than
thought.

The blissful couple, now with rice prominently adorned everywhere
from Tammy's hair to Mecot's shoes, made it to Rover. Mecot, the gen-

tleman, escorted Tammy to the passenger side and opened the door, then kissed her cheek (all the guests were sighing with jubilance at this point) and helped her into Rover. He proceeded to the driver side, waved good-bye, and kindly expressed his gratitude on behalf of himself and Tammy for everyone's love and support. He got in, rolled down the window, and shouted, "Ya'll are the best. Rat and I love you. Thanks again for giving us a great start!"

Rover was all decked out. You could hear the clicking and clanking of all the cans tied to the back of it. The white, silver, and gold streamers were hung from top to bottom and they were gently blowing against Rover's bright yellow exterior. Written on every window was the traditional phrase Just Married. Tammy's window was decorated with the word Rat and Mecot's window was decorated with the word Marine.

And as their wedding day came to an end, they drove down the hill and the guests returned to the garden for one last glass of champagne. So began Tammy and Mecot's new life.

We were led to believe they were going to the Coast to Coast Motel along the river just a few miles away. However, just as everyone was finishing their last glass of champagne, we all could hear a car horn blowing nonstop and turning up the driveway. It was Rover. Mecot and Tammy decided to come back and party with all their family and friends. Mecot pulled up and opened the door for Tammy, and everyone stood motionless. With their arms around each other, Mecot and Tammy kissed, and then Mecot uttered, "We love you guys too much and we will be heading to base tomorrow, so we wanted to hang out with you guys tonight if that's OK." Talk about a party. Daddy cranked up the music, ordered more food and beverages, and the reception lingered into the wee hours of the night.

Mecot and Tammy escorted the last guests down the hill to their cars. We were all exhausted and sitting comfy-cozy on the porch. Mecot gave a wink to us and softly whispered, "We have to get to our honeymoon now, pardon us." He picked Tammy up and carried her down the hill to the basement entryway of our home. My parents had hired the best carpenter in town to turn the unfinished basement into a separate living space complete with a large bedroom, bathroom, kitchen, and living room. Mecot carried her over the threshold, closed the door, and turned off the porch light. All I could hear was giggling for the next five minutes that soon turned into the stillness of this special night.

16

Life at Lejeune

IT WAS A LONG DRIVE THAT BEAUTIFUL DAY in May straight back to base at Camp Lejeune, North Carolina. They did not get to go on a honeymoon. Mecot's orders called for him to return to base immediately following their wedding day.

Together they trucked down the highway in the heavily decorated Rover, through the tunnels, over the mountain ranges, and into the heartland of one of the most well-known bases for the U.S. Marines. Mecot always used to kid around that he knew he was getting close to base when the roads became lined with tattoo shops and car dealerships.

Their home was very close to base too. They chose to live off base in a nice apartment complex with many other fellow Marine Corps families.

Weekends, when Mecot was not working, were fun times at their apartment community. He would hit the local convenience store on the way home and load up with plenty of beer and multiple bags of ice. Happy hour started right there at Tammy and Mecot's apartment.

He would load the bathtub with beers and bury them in ice. In no time, the neighbors were strolling over with trays of finger sandwiches and goodies to snack on. They sat up playing cards and sharing stories into the wee hours of the night. Occasionally, Mecot would whip out the ole banjo and play songs, with all his buddies singing along with him. As the night progressed, their singing became unrecognizable, but the wives completely got a kick out of their antics.

Mecot had great work hours and he and Tammy had plenty of time together. Sometimes they spent the time hanging out with neighbors. But
mostly they shared much alone time together. She shared with me some
of her fondest moments with him:

> He introduced me to the fishing hole, which quickly became
> "our fishing hole" as soon as we got there. We called it the
> "flounder hole" because we pulled a ton of flounder out of
> that water. It was located on base on one of the back roads.
> Between that place and fishing off the Onslow Fishing Pier, I
> felt like I was always on a honeymoon with him. Every day
> was so relaxing and enjoyable while we were fishing. And
> believe me, we fished almost every evening after dinner. We
> conceived little Mecot the first week in July. So we did make
> plenty of time for that stuff too!

As Tammy mentioned, when Mecot got off work they would usually
go fishing; however, when Mom and I were in town to visit the routine
changed so that we would all be able to spend time together.

I recall going to visit, and Tammy would have the apartment nicely
decorated, from lace curtains to floral-print bedspreads. She really created a lovely home.

Visits to their place were always fun-filled. My mom and I would road
trip there occasionally and stay for a few days. We did not want to stay too
long and impose on their newlywed life. It was great to hang out with
Tammy, just like old times. We would load up in Rover and go shopping.

Shopping was a little different because there was not a shopping mall
or large department store near the base. So our shopping outings led us
to the PX, the post exchange, which is similar to a department store but
located on a military base for military families to shop at discounted
prices. I loved when Tammy took me there. We shopped for hours looking at clothes, shoes, makeup, and perfumes. It wasn't the mall setting

with a wide variety of shops, but it was still fun. We would act silly, trying on different hats, pretending to be famous movie stars. We hadn't missed a beat from when we used to see each other almost every day back home in Hinton.

On one of my visits, Mecot had just found out I decided to run track for our high school team. Our high school had just started the track program a few years after Mecot and Tammy graduated. I figured it would help me maintain my girlish figure when I was not cheering for football or basketball season. I loved jumping hurdles. Mecot would always joke with me and tell me I must have little frog legs to get across the hurdle. He thought they looked so high up compared to my five foot two and a half stature. Not only was I the hurdle queen, but I also ran the one hundred yard dash, a race that required a lot of conditioning.

So Mecot thought it would be very brotherly to help me condition for the one-hundred-yard dash and build up some of my endurance. We put on our sneakers, hopped in Rover, and drove to the track on base. It was great. He really pushed me along. It seemed like he was the Energizer Bunny. He just kept going and going and going. And I was slowing and slowing and slowing.

We talked along the way. He asked me about my current love life. The "love of my life" at the time had decided to break up with me the previous week. It was an on-again, off-again kind of relationship.

Mecot was the ultimate protector even if he was miles away. He wanted to know that I was OK back home, that no one was taking advantage of me or hurting me. I let him know I cried many sleepless nights over my on-again, off-again boyfriend. His name was Danny and Mecot knew him well. Mecot liked that he hunted and fished. They had immediately bonded. That old saying about how you want to end up with someone with the same morals and character like your dad or brother is so true. And I had felt Danny was the perfect fit. But in between my panting and Mecot's cadences, I let my brother know the relationship obviously wasn't meant to be.

Mecot stopped running. So I figured I better stop running too. He looked at me straight in the eyes and said adamantly, "Do not ever let a boy bring you to tears. You are a Camara, and we Camaras are strong—not insecure. Be proud of our name and know that with it comes strength and perseverance. Your heart may be broken now but it will soon mend. Trust me."

And away he ran, looking back and shouting, "Come on, li'l sister, you can't quit now! Keep moving—you're a Camara. Move it, move it!" And I thought to myself, "Wow, being a Marine is the perfect job for my brother." I barely made it around the last stretch.

The distance between us was getting greater and greater. Mecot was running faster and I was running slower. He finally slowed down enough for me to meet up with him. He knew I was completely done. I couldn't move another muscle. Mecot stooped down and said, "Hop on, li'l sister. I've got ya!"

I kind of laughed and panted, whispering, "I'm heavy and we still have a few more laps." He sternly shouted, "Hop on!" I uttered, "OK, but I do not want to hurt your back." He laughed again. I hopped on his back. And yes, he piggybacked me all the way to Rover. We were both laughing and screaming all the way. He actually started running with me on his back. I thought for sure he was going to drop me.

Mom and Tammy saw Rover pull in and Mecot come to my side. They thought I was hurt. He also piggybacked me to the apartment and we were just laughing beyond hysteria. Once Mom and Tammy figured I was not hurt but completely exhausted, they started to laugh with us. And so did some of the other neighbors too! They all knew Mecot and his gregarious personality.

Soon we had a little gathering of their friends by their front door laughing right along with us. Mecot graciously offered them a beer and introduced Mom and me to everyone. It was really nice because he had already spoken about us to his neighbors and a few of them chuckled and nonchalantly said, "She's just like you described." I can only imagine his description of me.

About that time Mecot's best friend from the Marine Corps, Butch, pulled up to park next to their apartment. Mecot and Tammy had invited him to dinner. The entire dinner Mecot was making innuendo about Butch and me dating one day. Mecot was quick to try to remedy my heartbreak.

As kindhearted as my brother was to try and set me up with Butch, I could not entertain the thought. My broken heart needed more time to heal. But hanging out with Butch and the family was a great distraction. You could see he and Mecot had a special connection. And that night I grew very fond of Butch.

Butch is a character. He always wears a smile that is just infectious. It is very similar to Mecot's smirky grin; however, Butch's smile is borderline obnoxious in that it's just huge. Although Butch has a small to medium stature, he stands tall and proud: a true Marine. What he lacks in height, he makes up for with his high energy and sense of humor. He's the type of man who can bring out a smile or a laugh in you even on your worst day.

It was not uncommon for Mecot and Butch to banter back and forth about all kinds of subjects from fishing and Mecot's stories of the big one that got away to relationships and how girls are nothing but trouble. But that evening they were outnumbered by three females and they knew they were walking on thin ice.

Butch and Mecot were in the kitchen throwing punches and kicks at each other. They were getting in Tammy's way while she was cooking, but she would just laugh at them. Mom and I watched with disbelief that these grown men, Marines, were so high-spirited with each other. They were true brothers at heart. Being in the Marines is a true brotherhood. That saying that brothers don't always have to have the same last name definitely applies to Mecot and Butch.

Butch was among many of Mecot's brothers at Camp Lejeune. For instance, one time Mecot had a few of his buddies help him out on a little mission. He decided he wanted to camouflage Rover and alerted his Marine brothers that he needed them to report to the vehicle maintenance building after work. He did not tell them why. Of course, his loyal comrades rose to the occasion. As requested, the fellow Marines he called upon had arrived before him and were waiting patiently. Mecot had planned it that way. Within a matter a minutes, in marched Mecot. They always joked they could see him from a distance because of his "high and tight" horseshoe haircut. He wore it with pride and he made sure each hair was cut to the exact specifications to be acknowledged as an official horseshoe haircut. It just fit his gregarious personality perfectly. He marched in and advised them of the mission: "This afternoon Rover is getting a makeover. I am pulling her in and we're going to morph her from sunshine-yellow into concealed camouflage." His friends were completely on board.

And in a few short hours Mecot's bright yellow jeep turned camouflage. You would never have known Rover was originally the shade of the brightest yellow sunny day ever. Rover had now been transformed; it had the ability to blend into the environment when out in the woods or on the back roads to Mecot and Tammy's favorite flounder hole.

17

From Fishing Hole to Family

I GOT TO SEE THE NEW ROVER A FEW MONTHS LATER when Mecot decided to come home for a long weekend. Tammy had already come a few weeks earlier since she knew that Mecot was going on "float" for a while. Float is what Mecot used to call the time that he was at sea doing maneuvers, and it refers to a battalion of Marines stationed in different areas of the world ready for combat if needed.

She wanted to be home with family, especially since she was getting close to her delivery date.

Needless to say, I had already heard from Tammy that Rover had a complete makeover. But I was still shocked when I saw Mecot pull up our driveway. There was not one sign of the old bright yellow sun-kissed Rover anywhere. The jeep was now a camouflaged work of art.

Mecot came home primarily to see Daddy. He had been diagnosed with lymphoma cancer a few months earlier and was undergoing the latest in cancer treatment at the time—chemotherapy. It was brutal. We drove to Johns Hopkins Hospital in Baltimore, Maryland, every few weeks for his treatment. We stayed for a week and then we drove the winding roads back home. Daddy would be in the back lying down, trying to rest and stay as comfortable as possible. He could not help but throw up on occasion. I could see in his eyes that he was always so anxious to get home. It was a difficult time.

It seemed like cancer was getting the better of our Daddy, although he was putting up a great fight. He kept smiling through it all. You really should have seen his smile when he saw Mecot coming through the front door for that weekend. I had Daddy sitting in his recliner lifting soup cans to stay strong. We did not have weights to lift at the time, so I improvised.

Living in a remote small town in West Virginia sometimes limited what we could purchase. No weights were sold at Murphy's Mart, which was our only department store in town. But I was determined to not let cancer take my Daddy. And Mecot was determined too.

He came in with his warm, smirky grin and it didn't take long until we were all smiling too! His smile was contagious! Daddy hopped out of his recliner and threw the cans of soup at the couch. Mecot said with a chuckle, "What's with the soup cans? Maybe I should incorporate it into a new training regimen for the recruits." Daddy laughed so hard he said his abs were going to explode. Daddy gleefully said, "It's your li'l sister's training regimen for me. Maybe the Marine recruits need a good strong dose of Little Sergeant Camara to whip them into shape!"

Daddy stood right beside Rat and her growing belly. Daddy rubbed her belly and chuckled, saying, "Rumor has it Camp Lejuene has a great flounder hole." I had mentioned this story to him one night while he was in Johns Hopkins undergoing chemotherapy.

Mecot couldn't get to Rat quick enough after picking up Daddy and giving him a big bear hug. Daddy was all of five foot four inches tall and not too heavy for his Marine son to lift.

Next in line for a big Mecot bear hug was Rat. However, Mecot laughed and expressed that something had literally come between them and he felt a little nervous picking her up. So they hugged a very gentle hug and Mecot laid a sweet, gigantic kiss on her lips.

Afterward, Mecot leaned over and gave her belly a big kiss too! He whispered, "Hello in there!" We all laughed until we cried. Yes, my American brother, my big brother, an official sergeant in the United States Marine Corps, was home for a few days.

I had seen him come through that door at least ten times a day growing up. He came in with fishing poles, BB guns, toy army soldiers, neighbor friends, football friends, fishing buddies, and fraternity brothers, and more recently, with friends from the Marines. I just loved when he walked through that door. I looked up to him so much and I loved when he was home and we could all spend time together.

I knew at a very young age that Mecot had a calling to serve others. He gallantly served and protected so many of us in our little town on a daily basis. It's only fitting that the Marine Corps replied back with a greater calling for Mecot to serve and protect our country. I would know of none more devoted, more willing, and more proud than my brother Mecot to answer that call and live a life as a Marine.

That evening Daddy insisted on a big Filipino dinner to celebrate Mecot's homecoming. Of course, Daddy called his sisters into action to whip up a delicious meal composed of chicken adobo, pancit, and egg rolls. Rat was at the end of her pregnancy and just the mention of Filipino food put a huge smile on her face. Mecot laughed again, "So this eating for two thing really happens, huh? Rat, honey, your smile shows me you could eat a cow right now." She rubbed her belly and whispered in his ear, "Absolutely!"

My aunts came over immediately following a huge shopping run to Kroger grocery. Mecot helped carry in multiple bags of groceries. They bought everything from fresh garlic to chicken to jasmine rice. Straight to the kitchen they went with their goodies and infectious high energy. Tammy, Threase, Mom, and I would act as the prep crew. All the fresh chopping and dicing of the celery, garlic, parsley, and carrots was tantalizing. Our entire home smelled like the best, freshest Filipino restaurant Hinton, West Virginia, had ever encountered.

They drank wine, chopped, diced, and kept each other entertained the entire afternoon. Dad was entertained with Mecot's playing the banjo on the patio with a mouthful of Beech-Nut chewing tobacco. Of course, Mecot's favorite.

We all gathered around the dining room table for the meal. I had the job of setting the table. I loved this job because I loved Mom and Dad's favorite china. Noritake Progression china in the blue moon pattern was gorgeous. The pattern was composed of green leaves and blue flowers intertwined on each plate, bowl, and serving dish. It always reminded me of springtime in the mountains. But most especially, it meant having family dinners together.

Mecot was thrilled to be having a family dinner too! He did not complain about the food or dining atmosphere with the Marine Corps, but we could all tell he was completely delighted with our family feast!

Our dining experience at the Camara home was a adventure. Daddy led us in our Catholic dining prayer. That was the only time there was any silence at our table. Within a matter of seconds complete chaos broke out: "Pass this," "Pass that," "Yum," "Delicious," "Tasty," and so on. We Camaras had no problem with descriptive words when it came to food, and although my aunts were still learning to speak grammatically correct, they shouted out in Filipino slang all the way through dinner. And a lot of times they would just nod and hold their glass of wine up and smile. Daddy always taught us smiling is a universal language. My aunts smiled. We smiled back. They laughed. We laughed back.

Mecot's presence sure seemed to perk Daddy up, and for that we were all thankful. As the town doctor, Daddy kept crazy hours when we were growing up—from making house calls to emergency surgeries—but somehow he always managed to make time for the three of us. And family dinner was never to be missed.

Growing up, Mecot's time with Daddy included lots of fishing. Mecot would catch the fish and Daddy would skin and clean them. They would walk down to the river on weekend mornings to fish. They would bring back their catch and clean and descale them. Well, Daddy would descale them. Mecot walked away from the task. He always said if he caught them Daddy would descale and clean them. And that Daddy did.

Mecot would fire up the grill. Mom would make rice and fresh vegetables from our neighbor's garden next door. We would always have rice at every meal. We could be having Pizza Hut pizza and salad but we would still have rice too. It was just a Filipino staple that Daddy was used to, and he passed this tradition on to Mecot, Threase, and me.

But that evening's dinner was complete Filipino-style. Filipinos are notorious for their hospitality. My aunts kept loading up all our plates. Daddy always said, "Eat, eat! Food is love!" Wow, we were all feeling the love and we were all feeling very, very full by the end of our dinner.

Everyone pitched in to clean up. It was so much fun. I did sneak away for a few minutes to play the piano. I thought it would motivate the cleaning crew, composed of the women and Mecot and Ron, my sister's husband. Daddy sat in the living room watching me and laughing, because while I was playing my aunts were trying to sing the words to the songs.

After the dishes were done, we all hung out in the "orange room." That is what we named our family room. When Daddy had the addition done, he put bright orange shag carpet in there, so it became known as the orange room.

Aunt Era and Aunt Gemma got the guitars out for a little after-dinner singing session. I don't know how they could sing at the top of their lungs after that huge meal, but they managed to do it. I could see after their third performance that Daddy was looking tired and so was Rat.

We all decided it was time to say our prayers as a family as we did every night. We kneeled down in our hallway facing the miniature grotto that Daddy created with the Blessed Mary. We said our prayers together and we all went to our bedrooms to sleep.

Daddy and Mom slept downstairs in the guest room. They gave up their bedroom for Mecot and Rat to sleep in. She was full term and they wanted her to be as comfortable as possible.

I went to my bedroom after Mecot gave me a good-night bear hug. I was so full I shouted, "Don't squeeze too hard, unless you want another helping of pancit delivered straight from my stomach!" He squeezed anyway and ran away while laughing hysterically.

I brushed my teeth, washed my face, and went to my bedroom. It could not have been more girly. Daddy had gone with me to buy Flare

Squares at Murphy's Mart a few months earlier. I had pink-flowered
Flare Squares on every wall and a white canopy bed complete with pink
sheer curtains and a flowered bedspread. It was complete with pink shag
carpet and a gorgeous sparkly white ornate chandelier.

My dresser and nightstand matched my bed. And the curtains matched my
pink bedspread perfectly. We had ordered it from the Sears catalog years
ago. My pink phone, with my own phone line, was by my bed too. My bedroom was my sanctuary. After a crazy-busy night celebrating Mecot's homecoming, I was ready for a good sleep. That was the plan anyway....

I thought I was having a nightmare because I was hearing screams coming from Dad and Mom's bedroom. The screams were so real I sat up,
wondering if I was in a dream or if I was in reality. The screams would
stop and I'd settle down. The screams would start and I would sit up, confused. The third go-around I knew it was real. I was so scared. All I could
think was that someone had broken in the house and was hurting Mom or
Tammy because it was a female scream.

I slowly climbed out of bed, locked my door, and put my ear against it. I
heard nothing for a long time and then I heard it again. This time it was
even more piercing. How could this be? If someone broke in they never
would have made it past my big brother. He was a Marine. Good luck trying to take him down. But who would break in and why?

I gathered up the courage to unlock the door and see where the
screams were coming from. I slowly tiptoed to the hallway. At that moment I heard the worst scream ever coming from Mom and Dad's bedroom. I shouted, "Hey, is everything OK in there?" I had goose bumps
running down my spine and I was shaking horribly. I slowly opened the
door just enough to peek in.

I shouted, "Oh God!" Mecot exclaimed, "Yes, everything is OK! Go get
Mom and Dad. Rat is in labor. The baby's coming." I closed the door. I ran
downstairs. Mom and Dad were sound asleep and Daddy was quite weak
from his chemo and tired from our busy day with the family.

I shouted, "Help! Help! Mecot and Rat need you now! She is in labor.
She is screaming in pain!" I only had to say it once, and they were amaz-

ing. Daddy (the doctor) and Mom (the nurse) went to the rescue. Although Daddy was weak, he somehow mustered the strength to run up the stairs right behind Mom.

"Oh my God!" shouted Mecot. "Do something!" Rat was screaming bloody murder. At that moment, her screams were enough to scare me away from any future thought of being with the opposite sex and getting pregnant for a very, very long time!

Daddy told Mecot to go start up Rover. We would all help her. Mecot said an adamant, "NO! I've got my wife. You guys go start Rover." Mom ran down the hallway, out the back door, and climbed into Rover. Dad and Mecot helped Rat get in. After they were all loaded, I followed them there. I had my flashers going the entire way. It was only three miles down the road, but it seemed more like fifty. It was a direct path into the Summers County Hospital and straight to the emergency room.

Mecot was completely focused on Rat. He was calm, cool, and collected, although he could hardly stand her being in so much pain. He kept telling Dad to do something to make her pain go away. Daddy let him know soon enough the pain would slow down and he would be holding his beautiful baby.

Daddy delivered most all the babies from the late 1960s through the 1980s in Hinton. If anyone knew how to deliver healthy babies into this world, Daddy was the professional. He would remind us on occasion that delivering babies was one of the best parts of being a doctor.

In all the chaos, Daddy mentioned to Mecot that Tammy was in the best of hands and he wasn't leaving her side. Daddy and Tammy's primary obstetrician, a well-respected female doctor named Dr. Dani, were prepping for Tammy's delivery.

Daddy tried to comfort Mecot, and so he made sure to remind him that Crista, Threase and Ron's first child, was delivered right there as well. She bounced into this world healthy and happy. Daddy gave Mecot a big hug and said, "Let's go, son. It's time to make you a daddy!"

So several hours later, with Mecot by her side, her mom and my mom at the head of her bed, and Daddy and the nurse at the opposite end of the bed, Tammy was told to take a deep breath and start pushing. The pushing did not end for what seemed an eternity. I knew throughout this whole experience that Daddy was so thrilled to be delivering his own grandchild and his only son's baby. He was the on-call physician, father, and soon-to-be grandfather all in one that blustery night. His smile exuded sheer bliss. He was doing what he loved to do with the people who mattered most in the world to him.

Finally, I could hear Daddy coaching Tammy: "One more big push! This is it! Deep breath in! Exhale and push with all your might!"

The next sound was their new baby boy crying a healthy, boisterous cry. Daddy cut the umbilical cord and handed Mecot the baby. Mecot brought him around to Rat and placed him on her chest. He kissed her cheek and whispered in her ear, "You done good, my sweet wife. Ten fingers and ten toes. He is the most beautiful, healthy baby boy ever!" Rat was exhausted. They don't call it labor for nothing.

So Mecot came out to share the good news. He looked exhausted and exhilarated all at the same time. My brother-in-law, Ron, gave him a big hug and handshake and looked him in the eye. "Welcome to parenthood, my brother. It's a wild ride!" My sister gave him a big squeeze and I did too! All I could think was wow, my brother, a U.S. Marine, a husband, a brother, a son, and now a father rolled into one amazing young man. It was March 29, 1982, when Mecot and Rat's life would change forever. Welcome Mecot Echo Camara, Jr.

Mecot and Tammy wanted to name him Echo. However, this was not a name of which Daddy approved. He repeatedly advised them to change the name to something from the Bible. Daddy explained to them that "Echo" is nowhere in the Bible; however, Mecot, Sr. adamantly conveyed that at the moment, he was the only legacy to our family name. Not to mention, Mecot and Tammy decided on that name together on a special wintery night.

So the news spread quickly in our little all-American town and before you knew it, townsfolk were dropping off homemade crocheted baby

Mecot swinging with baby Echo at our family home with Sunshine, the family dog, next to them. Sunshine missed Mecot went he went to boot camp and quite often would lay by his bedroom door awaiting his return.

blankets, booties, sweaters, and quilts. They were all lovely works of art with beautiful pastel shades of blue, soft lace, and fancy ribbons. For Tammy, homemade apple butter, jams, jellies, and fresh garden vegetables to help her regain her strength were being dropped off by the droves.

Seeing everyone eager to help, from our next-door neighbors to folks coming down from the mountaintops, was so compelling to me. Out of nothing but sheer delight and gratitude for the things that Daddy (the town doctor) and Mecot (the helpful boy next door) had done for the community, these kindhearted folks selflessly chose to be generous enough to share their food and homemade gifts with Mecot and Rat.

It was within a very few short days that Mecot and Rat had decided to fulfill the Camara tradition and celebrate Echo's baptism at St. Patrick's Catholic Church. Echo wore our family baptismal gown, which was hand-made from nuns in the Philippines. It was made from one hundred percent pineapple lace. It was an heirloom that had been handed down through the Camara family for years.

The baptism was a beautiful ceremony. Mecot and Rat carried Echo up to the altar and stood beside the priest and the baptismal font. After the reading of the Catholic baptismal rites, Rat took off Echo's lace bonnet and gently leaned his head into the font. Father Tedesco poured the holy water over his forehead and blessed him.

Echo was very quiet through the entire Mass up to this point, but once the water came over his head he let the entire congregation know of his presence. Let's just say he was a very healthy baby boy who had been blessed with a great set of lungs.

The Camara family had never been short of passion and, on that day, we were all sitting in the front pew with tears of joy streaming down our cheeks.

18

Emergency Return Home

OUR TEARS OF HAPPINESS FOR THE BIRTH of Echo turned to tears of melancholy. Mecot had to transform back into a U.S. Marine shortly and head back to float. He was stationed in the Mediterranean Sea.

Although it would be difficult for Tammy having Mecot leave, she knew she would be OK at home in Hinton with her family and Echo to keep her busy. But for Daddy, it would be another story.

We all knew it would be hardest on Daddy because he sensed in his heart that it might be one of the last times he would be with Mecot. Mecot gave him a big hug and told him to keep fighting. Mecot said, "We Camaras are not quitters. We do not give up. Daddy, you taught us this. Now you have to live by it to survive. You can do it. I'll be sending you lots of letters for your reading enjoyment!"

Daddy did not give up. He did go into remission for a couple of months. He even got to go back to work and performed some surgeries until he became too weak and his hands started to shake. At that point, he knew it was time to stop practicing surgeries.

The good news was that Mecot did not have to leave right away from Camp Lejuene, and for the next few months, daily life continued for Rat, Mecot, and Echo. Mecot still had great work hours that allowed him to spend much time with his family. Many evenings were spent on the Onslow Fishing Pier.

He would pack up Echo and bring his playpen, baby bottles, and diaper bag. He set up the playpen on the pier between him and Tammy. They were all set with fishing poles, gear, bait, and cooler. They had this routine down pat.

Although it took the locals a little getting used to, they would witness Mecot's little family as they marched down the pier in full force. Mecot would set up the playpen, place Echo in it with a bottle, bait the fishing pole for Rat, and grab a beer out of the cooler. And before you knew it, Mecot had befriended every one of those skeptical local fishermen who thought Mecot and his family were completely unconventional.

⚓

A few months passed. Mecot had gone back to sea, writing home frequently. When a letter arrived, I would use it to motivate Daddy to exercise. When we were done exercising, I would read his letter from Mecot. Daddy loved getting letters from Mecot. He would don a large smile after each letter I would read to him. I continued directing Daddy in his soup-can exercises from his recliner every day.

One day I decided to go hit some tennis balls at Bellepoint Park. Daddy was resting and Mom was taking care of him. I was at the concession stand when Karen Williams, one of our neighbors, approached me. She said, "I have to take you to the hospital. Your mom had Pru (that's what all the neighbors called him) transported to the hospital, and he is not doing well."

I knew what was coming but I did not want to accept it. I was sixteen years old. Sixteen-year-old girls are not supposed to have their fathers die. I kept thinking in my head over and over, *This cannot be happening.*

Karen walked me into the hospital. The same hospital in which Daddy had saved lives, birthed babies, and stitched up every neighbor kid's open wounds. And now I was walking through those doors to say goodbye to him. Who was going to save him? *Who works here that is going to save him today?*

It was a very long walk down the corridor to his room. I took a deep breath, held in my tears, then walked in and gave him a hug. He told me he was going to be watching me from heaven and that I had to be a good girl or he was going to drop a rock on my head. He made me laugh and cry all at the same time.

I stayed with him. I was not leaving his side that afternoon. Mom had gone home for a few minutes, but my aunts were there. We took turns swabbing his lips with Vaseline to keep them moist. He was coming in and out of consciousness. His breathing became very shallow. He took his last breath a few minutes before midnight.

I became hysterical. My brother-in-law Ron's parents took me down to the emergency room, where they tried to give me a shot to calm down. I kicked and screamed, "NO! It will only delay my pain. Get that shot away from me! Leave me alone now! No shot is going to bring back my dad or make my pain go away." I was young but I was not stupid. The ER nurse did not give me that shot. Instead she and Ron's parents just sat with me and let me cry. They consoled me for what seemed like hours.

Daddy passed May 7, 1982. We all needed Mecot to come home. We were pretty much nonfunctioning for the next few days. Tammy called Camp Lejuene and let them know what happened, but they could not get Mecot off the ship. My mother called as far up the ranks of the Marine Corps as possible, but they could not bring him home.

Mom's last call was to Senator Robert Byrd. He and Daddy had become close friends over the years. When Senator Byrd would come through Hinton campaigning, he would always come to our home. There were many walks through Daddy's garden with Senator Byrd. I never knew what a politician and a doctor could chat about, but I do know they had a deep respect for each other.

Mom spoke with the Senator personally. He was deeply saddened by Daddy's death. Mom let him know we needed Mecot home and that we were not making any headway with the commanding officers. Senator

Byrd told Mom he would be in touch within twenty-four hours. Do not make final arrangements yet, he said.

Senator Byrd did call back and it was definitely less than twenty-four hours. He told us that they were sending a helicopter to the ship and transporting Mecot back to base. From there Mecot and Rover made the trip back home. He pulled up in our driveway three days after Daddy's death.

Mecot was our rock. I guess Daddy missed my head and dropped the rock within feet of me in the form of my big brother. He must have known I was going to need Mecot's strength. There was hardly room for Mecot to park in the driveway because there were cars everywhere as people poured in, sharing their hugs and sorrow with us.

I saw him first and my eyes began filling with tears. He ran through the door and we all started screaming and crying. Mom was shouting, "Now what, now what, now what...what do I do?" Tammy and li'l Echo were standing there in disbelief. She missed him so much but she was not expecting to be with him under these circumstances. Mecot kissed Rat and reached for li'l Echo and calmly gazed into everyone's eyes as he quietly expressed his sadness.

He asked that we all take a moment to remember Daddy and know that he would not want us here together screaming and crying. He would want us here together remembering him and how he lived each day as a kind, humble, and caring man. Mecot said softly, "I'm home. Let's all be together and take it one step at a time for the next few days."

Mecot's presence was what the doctor ordered: heaven-sent, of course, direct from Daddy up above. We buried my father at Restwood Cemetery on the very top of the mountain. Our family and town came together to honor my father. My father: the town doctor, team physician, school board member, neighbor, and friend to all.

Mecot was now our family leader. He was the cohesiveness that kept us all together. Immediately following the burial, however, he was ordered back to Camp Lejeune to work in the office until his platoon returned from being on float.

But while he was home in Hinton, we all felt blessed for the time that he could be with us. He left giving us the support and strength to keep moving forward.

He would remind me, "You are marching forward one step at a time and you are not stopping to look back—march, march, march onward and upward." He would call it out in cadence to me: "March—march—march—forward—march—march—march—do—not—stop—do—not—look—back—march—march—march!" He said he'd be back soon enough but in the meantime I should help Mom around the house, study hard, and stay away from boys. Mecot and his little family left and I cried big tears that day too!

⁂

Mecot was right. Life moves on. Threase and Ron went back to their daily lives with little Crista and their soon-to-be new addition arriving in October. And I went back to finish my junior year at Hinton High School.

It was just Mom and I living in our home. It was so quiet. I would walk down the hill often to hang out at Threase's home just to escape the quiet from our big house. And I was always having my girlfriends over too! Mom would make us dinner and we'd hang out and watch movies. On game nights, I would have all the cheerleaders over. We would do each other's hair and makeup and Mom would make us her infamous fried chicken. Then we would catch the bus at the end of our driveway and go off to cheer on the Hinton Bobcats football team.

Life did continue. Aside from trying to be a normal sixteen-year-old girl minus the coolest dad ever, and minus the coolest big brother ever, I hung out with my friends, shopped, and did typical teenage stuff. But one of my favorite things to do on Saturday mornings was to drive my jade-green Buick Regal with the T-tops off to the post office in downtown Hinton where I would park and run straight to our mailbox.

Every Saturday, I looked for a letter from Mecot. When one came in the entire post office would know! I would jump up and down shouting,

"I got one today!" Eventually the entire post office staff knew exactly what my happy dance was all about. They remembered it from Mecot's letters coming to me from boot camp in Parris Island, South Carolina.

My world was so sheltered in my small town of Hinton. I had no idea that Mecot's future mission would send him halfway around the world to the unstable region of Beirut, Lebanon. In the summer of 1982, at the request of the Lebanese government, the United States agreed to establish a U.S. military presence in that country to serve as a peacekeeping force in the conflict between warring Muslim and Christian factions.

19

Peacekeepers at Risk

T HE FOLLOWING ARTICLE, BY RETIRED U.S. Air Force Lieutenant Colonel Edward Marek, highlights almost month-by-month the worsening aggression in Beirut and what the Twenty-Fourth Marine Amphibious Unit was dealing with while serving as peacekeepers there—from the moment they landed.

'24th MAU Arrives in Beirut, 1-8 Marines Embarked'

The 24th MAU arrived on May 29, 1983, to conduct a relief in place for the 22nd MAU. Col. Timothy Geraghty now commanded the 24th. BLT 1-8 Marines had replaced BLT 3-8, Lt. Col. Howard Gerlach, in command.

The first 24th MAU Marines came ashore on May 28, 1983, moved into positions at the airport, and began mobile and foot patrols around the airport and US and UK embassies. Like the previous MAUs, the 24th HQ was set up at the fire fighter school at the airport and BLT 1-8 set up at the four-story building used by the other BLTs.

The patrols continued, at the rate of about 4–7 patrols per day around the airport. Reinforcing all positions continued. LAF fire teams accompanied the Marines on their patrols outside the airport. The situation in Lebanon continued to deteriorate. As a result, Geraghty started planning for operations to the south as the LAF replaced the departing Israelis, should that happen.

On July 22, 1983, the airport was attacked by local militias employing guns, rockets, and mortars. One Sailor and two Marines were slightly injured. At month's end, a small group of gunmen fired with semi-automatic weapons at Marines through the airport fence while they were jogging. No one was hit. The 24th continued training the LAF and other MNF units.

Rocket barrages against the airport resumed on August 8, hitting between the MAU and BLT headquarters and the LAF flight line and camps. Then, during the early morning hours of August 9, rockets exploded around Marine positions, [and] the Marines returned fire using mortars—the first time the Marines would employ indirect fire since they first came to Lebanon as part of the MNF.

The Marines launched two Cobra helicopters with orders to attack if they found targets. Offshore ships were put on general quarters and prepared to fire. The airport remained closed through August 16. It was occasionally hit by rockets. A few Marines were wounded. The Marines remained the targets of small-scale harassment without major injury.

Militia fighting was now heavy in the hills above the airport and in the city, with [fighting] becoming intense around the airport in late August and early September. The Marines received fire at the airport and at their positions at the Lebanese University. On August 29, rocket fire into the airport was very heavy, one every 15 seconds.

The USS *Belknap* (CG-26) fired two illumination rounds at militia positions, which did not stop the rockets. The Marines decided to respond with 155 mm high-explosive point-detonating artillery, silencing the militia.

Incredibly, an unidentified armored vehicle opened fire on a LAF-Marine checkpoint employing .50 caliber and 7.62 mm machine guns. Two Cobra gunships were tasked to locate the source. The armored vehicle then fired at the Cobras. The Cobras replied and shut down the enemy fire. One Cobra took three hits and made an emergency landing on the Iwo Jima.

On August 30, the LAF swept through west Beirut and the resulting engagements threatened the UK-US embassy. Heavy fighting resumed. An antitank squad from BLT 1-8 went over to the embassy to beef up the security there, their convoy escorted by helicopter. Marine positions at the airport and the university were now under attack. The Marines returned fire as well as they could give their ROEs.

The last three days of August were marked by persistent militia attacks from the hills east of the airport. The Marines found it hard to determine who was who. U.S. Army personnel at the ministry of defense came under fire. The Marines replied with 155 mm howitzers.

Based on all the activity described during the end of August, the JCS prepared to reinforce the Marines and sent the USS *Eisenhower* Carrier Battle Group to the scene.

In the meantime, the Israelis, without warning anyone, began to withdraw from the south, forcing the LAF to move into areas of Beirut very hostile to it. They crossed Marine positions and their soldiers even became mixed with Marines. As a result, the Marines took fire and replied, where they could identify targets, with machine guns, small arms, and the main gun of one tank. This all went from bad to worse over the early days of September.

Militias were fighting against each other in the hills, fighting against the LAF from the hills, dissidents were fighting against the LAF in the city, and the Marines were caught in the middle of an unwieldy mess. Marine positions along the south of the airport were under constant attack, and they suffered minor injuries. Heavy rocket attacks began on September 5 and by September 6 some 120 artillery, mortar, and rocket rounds had struck that section of the airport. The Marines continued to employ their 155 mm howitzer to good effect.

With the arrival of the *Eisenhower*, a Navy F-14 Tomcat flew the first photo reconnaissance mission over enemy positions. There was a surface-to-air missile (SAM) threat but the Navy determined they could handle it.

The back-and-forth of all this continued…[I]n a situation like this, I suspect the Marines would have preferred to get some of their forces out of and away from the airport, even into the hills, if for no other reason than to reconnoiter. They found it hard to identify whom they should attack among the militias. The net result was they were forced into generally fixed positions, which they hate. I know Navy SEALs did some reconnaissance up in the hills, which was helpful.

In mid-September, the 31st MAU arrived with BLT 3-3 embarked. It was on its way back from an exercise in Kenya. The 31st was sent offshore Lebanon and prepared to be a contingency landing force. On September 16, the UK-US embassy came under heavy shelling. The USS Bowen and John Rodgers fired 72 rounds on six targets and silenced the enemy. Lebanese units were attacked by Palestinians in the hills, and requested naval fire on September 19. They got it from the USS *Virginia, John Rodgers, Bowen*, and *Radford.* Some 360 shells were fired over five hours and the Palestinians withdrew and broke contact. Arguably the most important political point here is that, indisputably, the Marines were no longer neutrals. They were in the fight on the side of the LAF. The Marines' mission had clearly changed. That made them legitimate targets for the enemy.

On September 20, two Navy reconnaissance aircraft were fired on by SA-7 shoulder-mounted SAMs. They missed by quite a margin. Naval offshore fire was now commonplace while the Marines remained at their checkpoints and positions around the airport, at the embassy, and at the university. The French commenced air strikes. Two Army soldiers were kidnapped, but released to the French. A Marine helicopter crashed at sea, both pilots rescued without injury.

Near month's end, the battleship USS *New Jersey* arrived.

A cease-fire was put in place, the airport was re-opened on September 30, and the Marines got some time off aboard ships for hot showers, good food, and some rest.

The cease-fire quickly began to unravel; Marine helicopters took hostile fire and received some damage. On October 8 heavy fighting broke out again, a few Marines were wounded by sniper fire, and a CH-46 helicopter was struck by two rounds piercing its skin. There could be no doubt that the Marines were considered enemy.

On October 12, 1983, General P. X. Kelley visited the Marines, and awarded 12 Purple Hearts. Incredibly, no Marines had been lost....

The Marines continued receiving hostile fire, helicopters continued to receive fire, most notably perhaps sniper fire, and one Marine was seriously wounded and [medivaced]. Marine snipers took the offense and silenced the enemy fire. Marines from A/1-8 Marines at the university received a serious attack on October 16, machine gun and rifles. A four-hour exchange occurred. Five rocket propelled grenades struck Marine positions and five were wounded. The enemy fire was so heavy a medivac helicopter was unable to land. The British provided a ground escort to get the most seriously wounded out. On October 19, a supply convoy was hit by a remote controlled car bomb. Four Marines were wounded.

It's now October 20 and 21, 1983, and the situation quieted. On October 22, a USO show did its thing at the BLT 1-8 headquarters. Everyone was excited to have the USO put on a show with live music and lots of singing. The 24th MAU was anticipating leaving in mid-November, and had already begun to prepare.[11]

In one of Mecot's letters to Rat, he told her how he was getting excited to be coming home that November. He was ready for a big Thanksgiving dinner at home in the mountains of West Virginia, where he would not be getting fired upon and where he could be with her and Echo and eat turkey, mashed potatoes, and pancit until he couldn't move. He said he could envision Echo with mashed potatoes all over his face and hands.

Tammy and I would talk regularly, even though I was in college in Charlotte and she was at Camp Lejuene with Echo and the other wives. We still managed to keep our close-knit relationship. I could envision her sitting at their apartment kitchen table feeding Echo in his high chair and talking to me with the long corded wall phone (at that time cordless phones did not exist), the sun beaming through their big kitchen window.

Mecot's letters never made us question his safety. He always reassured us that "there is nothing the U.S. Marines can't handle." Sometimes Rat would read me what Mecot wrote to her. It was the best romance novel ever. I could hear her smile through the phone as she'd read his words. Not only was he getting excited to be coming home soon, but Tammy was excited for it too—and so was the rest of the family!

---

[11] Reprinted with permission from Edward S. Marek, Lt. Col., USAF (Ret.), "Largest Non-Nuclear Explosion on Record Hits Beirut Marines, Twenty-Five Years Ago," Talking Proud (October 2008), available at http://www.talkingproud.us/Retired/Retired/BeirutMarines.html.

20

Presidential Comfort

O UR EXCITEMENT TURNED TO DEVASTATION and the dreary memorial service that I attended with the family did little to console our broken hearts. We were all missing our American brother.

Here is an excerpt from an article that epitomizes the ceremony our family attended.

It never got better on that Nov. 4, 1983, less than two weeks after 241 servicemen, most from Camp Lejeune and New River Air Station, were killed when a military outpost was bombed by terrorists in Beirut.

The day President Reagan visited Camp Lejeune to attend a memorial service for those killed in the Beirut bombing dawned stormy and dismal.

There was no sun. No blue sky. No rainbow. No promise that things would soon be better. Just a damp funk that enshrouded the entire community. The weather perfectly matched the attitude of those who attended the service.

"As we approached the traffic circle in the dark, the mood was set for the day with the simple words, 'In Memoriam' on the announcement sign across from base headquarters," said Bonnie Throckmorton, a longtime Jacksonville resident and regular contributor to the *Daily News.*

She vividly recalled the heavy downpour as Camp Lejeune Marines awaited the arrival of their commander-in-chief. "I remember watching the Marine uniforms turn from green to black as the water soaked in. The flags from all the base units formed the backdrop against the water. As they were whipping in the wind and rain, three helicopters came out of the darkness, flying just above the ground. We knew President Reagan had arrived," Throckmorton said.

From where the press sat during the service, many rows back from the raincoat-clad president, the world appeared as a sea of umbrellas. They mushroomed over the heads of guests, victims, and the reporters who tried to take notes during the short, but moving, memorial service.

Reagan came to honor the Camp Lejeune Marines and sailors killed on Oct. 23, an event that sent Jacksonville and Camp Lejeune into a tailspin.

In the hours and days that followed the bombing, Marines prepared to deploy to Beirut to assist in rescue efforts and provide additional security. Jacksonville would be besieged with media representatives. Reporters from the networks and national newspapers and magazines converged on the town, along with the international press corps. Gen. Al Gray, who commanded the Second Marine Division, to which the Beirut contingent was attached, held regular press briefings.

Jacksonville residents discovered the extent of their loss as confirmed casualty numbers climbed. So many of the men who perished were friends, neighbors, and integral parts of the community. Jacksonville, like the rest of the nation, looked to its president for both leadership and inspiration.

Reagan was popular in this conservative military town. Perceived as both pro-military and an able leader, most in Jacksonville felt that he was someone to take seriously in the world arena, a man who didn't bluff or back down from a fight. The kind of leader a fighting force such as the Marines could feel confident in following.

Glenn Hargett, who now works for the city of Jacksonville, was there for WJNC radio station, along with Ron Brown, the station's general manager. Throckmorton was there as a Marine wife. Hargett remembers the scrambling for passes to attend the memorial services, which were followed by a private meeting between Reagan and the families of those who died.

"The rain may have kept some away, but I have a distinct memory of local officials, chamber members, the faith community, and others waiting in long lines for the check in," Hargett said.

The press had arrived very early so their equipment could be searched. In those days, members of the Fourth Estate weren't really accustomed to such scrutiny—not like in a post-9/11 world. Bags, purses, cameras, recorders, and notebooks were carefully screened and reporters, photographers, and sound crews passed through metal detectors. The press was in an area far behind the president, who was distinguishable only by his khaki raincoat and the cadre of Secret Service agents flanking him. First Lady Nancy Reagan accompanied the president. Dressed in black, she hovered under a huge umbrella.

After their arrival from Cherry Point Air Station, the Reagans made their way through the crowd and shook hands with survivors of the blast who were seated on the front row. Many were in wheelchairs.

The ceremony was brief, but moving, and the president didn't speak. Hargett says the quote that resonated most with him came from one of the Navy chaplains at the service who observed, "You think that it would break the heart of God," in referring to the Marines who were lost in the bombing.

For Throckmorton, the most memorable and poignant moment was when a child's tiny voice cried out from the section in which the families were seated, "Where's my daddy?"

"Never let it be said Marines don't cry," Throckmorton said.[12]

I do not recall seeing much of the president on that chilling, rainy day at Camp Lejuene because I was so saddened and so focused on the wounded sitting in front of us. Some sat in wheel chairs. Some were wrapped in bandages. And a few had bruises and black eyes. My heart broke for each and every one of them. All I could do was focus on them and what they lived through and, most especially, the horrible images that will never escape each of their minds.

However, later that afternoon President Reagan did speak at Cherry Point Marine Corp Air Station. Each word spoken compelled me to listen closer, as his words were passionate and compelling. President Reagan's speech follows.

Officers and men and women of the corps, ladies and gentlemen, I came here today to pay homage to the heroes of Lebanon and Grenada. We grieve along with the families of these brave, proud Americans who have given their lives for their country and for the preservation of peace.

I have just met with the families of many of those who were killed. I think all Americans would cradle them in our arms if we could. We share their sorrow. I want all of you

---

[12] Carole Moore, "President Shared Pain of Marine Community," Daily News (Jacksonville, NC), June 8, 2004. Reprinted with permission.

who lost loved ones and friends to know that the thoughts and prayers of this nation are with you.

If this country is to remain a force for good in the world, we'll face times like these, times of sadness and loss. Your fellow citizens know and appreciate those marines and their families are carrying a heavy burden.

America seeks no new territory, nor do we wish to dominate others. We commit our resources and risk the lives of those in our Armed Forces to rescue others from bloodshed and turmoil and to prevent humankind from drowning in a sea of tyranny.

In Lebanon, along with our allies, we're working hard to help bring peace to that war-torn country and stability to the vital Middle East. In seeking to stabilize the situation in Lebanon, you marines and sailors—and our French, Italian, and English companions—are peacekeepers in the truest sense of the word.

The world looks to America for leadership. And America looks to the men in its Armed Forces—to the Corps of Marines, to the Navy, the Army.

Freedom is being tested throughout the world. In Burma, that government has announced conclusive evidence of North Korean responsibility for the atrocity taking the lives of many members of the Korean government. We stand with South Korea, and I will be going there next week to carry our message to them, a message of revulsion of this atrocity, determination to stand with our friends in support of freedom.

In the Middle East this morning, we have learned of yet another terrorist assault similar to the attack against our marines, this time against an Israeli site in Tyre, Lebanon.

In spite of the complexity and special hardships of the Lebanese crisis, we have stood firm. As ever, leathernecks are willing to accept their mission and do their duty. This honest patriotism and dedication to duty overwhelms the rest of us.

In Grenada, our military forces moved quickly and professionally to protect American lives and respond to an urgent request from the Organization of Eastern Caribbean States. We joined in an effort to restore order and democracy to that strife-torn island. Only days before our actions, Prime Minister Maurice Bishop had been brutally murdered, along with several members of his cabinet and unarmed civilians. With a thousand Americans, including some eight hundred students, on that island, we weren't about to wait for the Iran crisis to repeat itself, only this time, in our own neighborhood—the Caribbean.

In a free society there's bound to be disagreement about any decisive course of action. Some of those so quick to criticize our operation in Grenada, I invite them to read the letters I've received from those students and their families. They know this was no invasion; they know it was a rescue mission. Marines have a saying—"We take care of our own." Well, America—with the help of marines—will take care of our own.

And our brave marines, soldiers, and Special Forces—including the truly gallant Navy Seals—were not just coming to the aid of our students. I hope every American will be able to hear the stories of the political prisoners who have been freed. The citizens of Grenada, who watched helplessly as their country was being stolen from them and turned into a staging area for totalitarian aggression—these same Grenadians are hailing us as liberators, and they're doing everything they can now to help. Every American can be proud of the professional and gallant job that our Armed Forces have done. And all of us can rejoice that they're coming home.

I came here today to honor so many who did their duty and gave that last, full measure of their devotion. They kept faith with us and our way of life. We wouldn't be free long, but for the dedication of such individuals. They were heroes. We're grateful to have had them with us.

The motto of the United States Marine Corps: "semper fidelis"—always faithful. Well, the rest of us must remain always faithful to those ideals which so many have given their lives to protect. Our heritage of liberty must be preserved and passed on. Let no terrorist question our will or no tyrant doubt our resolve. Americans have courage and determination, and we must not and will not be intimidated by anyone, anywhere.

Since 1775, marines, just like many of you, have shaped the strength and resolve of the United States. Your role is as important today as at any time in our history.

Our hearts go out to the families of the brave men that we honor today. Let us close ranks with them in tribute to our fallen heroes, their loved ones, who gave more than can ever be repaid. They're now part of the soul of this great country and will live as long as our liberty shines as a beacon of hope to all those who long for freedom and a better world.

One of the men in the early days of our nation, John Stuart Mill, said, "War is an ugly thing, but not the ugliest of things. The ugliest is that man who thinks nothing is worth fighting or dying for and lets men better and braver than himself protect him." You are doing that for all of us.

God bless you, and thank you for what you're doing.

Note: The president spoke at 12:06 p.m. at Cherry Point Marine Corps Air Station. Earlier, following his arrival at the air station, the president went to Camp Lejeune, where he attended a memorial service for those killed in Lebanon and Grenada and in honor of those wounded or missing. After the service, he went

*to the Second Marine Division Headquarters Building, where he
met with families of the honored dead.[13]*

⋘⊙⋙

Mom, Threase, Tammy, Echo, and I happened to fall in that latter cat-
egory: family of the honored dead. As we stood waiting in line to meet
the president and first lady, I gazed around at all the other "families of the
honored dead." They looked lifeless. Having the common bond of losing a
family member to a suicide bomber seemed surreal.

I recall standing there among mothers, fathers, wives, and children. All
with grief-stricken blank stares mixed between the cries of agony. There
was one lady a few places ahead of us, she must have been a mother, with
her head held low and sunken stature—she shook the president's hand and
said, "Why, why?" He hugged her and all I could see was him mouthing
the words, "I am so sorry for your loss." They moved all of us along at a
nice pace—not too quickly but not too slowly. Just long enough to meet
them. It was our turn next.

President Reagan gave me a firm handshake and gently touched my
other arm and very quietly whispered, "I am so sorry for your loss." I held
my composure as if Mecot were beside me and firmly shook his hand
back, and in somewhat of a daze I said, "Thank you."

I recall the first lady more vividly. Compared to the president, she was
very petite. We must have been close in height to each other. She looked
me right in the eye and could see me tearing up.

Mrs. Reagan whispered, "He must have been a very special big brother."
Somehow she knew I was a little sister to a special big brother. I tearfully
stated, "Yes, ma'am. He was my only brother. The best brother in the
world." She softly put her arms around me and hugged me. With a very

---

[13] Ronald Reagan, "Remarks to Military Personnel at Cherry Point, North Carolina, on the United States Casualties in Lebanon and Grenada" (speech, Cherry Point, NC, November 5, 1983), available at the Ronald
Reagan Presidential Library, http://www.reagan.utexas.edu/archives/speeches/1983/110483a.htm.

sweet, sincere expression, she whispered, "I am truly so sorry for your loss." I gently hugged her back and said, "Thank you very much, ma'am."

We were very much taken care of that day. We had escorts back to the limos and escorts to the airport. We had timed our visit so that we could fly back to West Virginia immediately after the ceremony. We left from the Jacksonville airport and flew directly into Charleston, West Virginia.

As we got close to Charleston, the mountains surrounded us. Most of the fall foliage was gone but that didn't matter to me on that particular gray, rainy day. I knew that Mecot would be resting peacefully atop one of them right beside Daddy. He would have wanted it that way. He loved growing up in these mountains. And it's only appropriate that his final resting place is high on a mountaintop, where, from a distance, it appears that heaven and earth meet.

21

Home at Last

November 1983
Hinton, West Virginia

A FTER WAITING FOR WHAT SEEMED LIKE MONTHS, my brother finally came home from the mountainous region of Beirut, Lebanon. He arrived just a few weeks before Thanksgiving. I was riding with the family as we followed him up the autumn-colored mountainside where he was to be buried beside our father.

We drove alongside the river, crossed over Madam's Creek Bridge, and up the curvy one-lane gravel road. We caravanned to Restwood Cemetery. It is a beautiful resting ground for my brother.

As we were driving past the river, my mind reflected on him and the rafting tours he led. I spent lots of time with him on that river, from fishing to rafting and canoeing. Mecot could never get enough of it during the summer months. His eyes would twinkle like the sun-kissed waters when he was on it.

Being outdoors was his ultimate high. I know God put us in the small town of Hinton for a reason. Growing up in a little valley nestled between the mountains, rivers, streams, and with a beautiful lake, made waking up every day a dream come true; most especially, for a little rambunctious boy name Mecot Camara.

As we were getting closer to the top of the mountain and nearer the cemetery, my mind drifted off to Mecot and this mountain we were climbing. This mountain was his playground. He picked blackberries with our Nanny here and he deer hunted and hiked with his buddies. It was only appropriate that he rest his soul here along this mountainside beside Daddy.

So we finally made it to his burial site. I did not want to get out of the limousine. I did not want to face the reality of burying my twenty-three-year-old big brother. The limousine driver opened the door. I could feel the cool, brisk air against my face. Not only was I chilled from the cool air on that colorful fall day, but I was also chilled from what the next few minutes ahead would mean to our family and our community.

The entire mountainside was covered with cars from the entrance all the way down to the bottom of the mountain. Hinton has a population of four thousand and on this day our family was completely surrounded by close to all four thousand Hintonians.

Seats were placed by Mecot's new resting place. Our family sat down and we held one another's hands. Tammy could not let go of their baby son, Mecot Echo.

The only thing in front of me was an empty, cold hole that Mecot was going to descend into. I could smell the freshly dug dirt and feel the moisture seeping up the earthen walls.

We sat quietly for what seemed an eternity as Mecot's friends, neighbors, teachers, coaches, and fraternity brothers gathered around us. I just kept watching them walking up the mountainside, one after another, with expressions of disbelief, shock, and sadness.

Mecot's pallbearers, consisting of eight US. Marines in their formal dress blues, marched together, carrying Mecot's flag-draped casket up the mountainside. I considered this to be Mecot's final march with his fellow Marine comrades.

They gently placed him on the metal braces above his burial site. They slowly removed his flag, and in ceremonial fashion they folded it and gave it to his widowed bride.

U.S. Marines carry the flag-draped coffin of Me- in Hinton. Camara died during an insurgent at-
cot E. Camara from St. Patrick's Catholic Church tack on command headquarters in Beirut.
                                                            Staff photo by John Blankenship

U.S. Marines carry the flag-draped coffin of Sgt. Mecot E. Camara from St.
Patrick's Catholic Church in Hinton. (Photo by John Blankenship of the
Beckley Register-Herald)

The priest performed Mecot's burial ceremony. I was fighting back the tears, trying to be strong, but at the same time all I could think about was my brother, having been killed senselessly—and here we are all together, our small American town, burying one of our own small-town heroes.

After the priest had finished with the traditional burial blessing, one of Mecot's high school friends came forward carrying his bugle and standing off to the side of the mountain. He began playing "Taps."

"Taps" has been most associated with military funerals, and there I sat listening to "Taps" at my brother's military funeral. According to Jari Villanueva, author of *Twenty-Four Notes That Tap Deep Emotions: The Story of America's Most Famous Bugle Call*, the most popular story regarding the tradition of the playing of "Taps" is about "a Northern boy who was killed fighting for the South [during the Civil War]. His father, Robert Ellicombe, a captain in the Union Army, came upon his son's body on the battlefield and found the notes to 'Taps' in a pocket of the dead boy's Confederate uniform. When Union General Daniel Sickles heard the story, he had the notes sounded at the boy's funeral. There is no evidence to back up the story or the existence of Captain Ellicombe...."

Villanueva continues,

> In July 1862, words were put with the music. The first were, "Go to Sleep, Go to Sleep." As the years went on many more versions were created. There are no official words to the music but here are some of the more popular verses:

> Day is done, gone the sun,
> From the hills, from the lake,
> From the sky.
> All is well, safely rest,
> God is nigh.

Go to sleep, peaceful sleep,
May the soldier or sailor,
God keep.
On the land or the deep,
Safe in sleep.

Love, good night, must thou go,
When the day, and the night
Need thee so?
All is well. Speedeth all
To their rest.

Fades the light; and afar
Goeth day, and the stars
Shineth bright,
Fare thee well; day has gone
Night is on.

Thanks and praise, for our days,
'Neath the sun, 'neath the stars,
'Neath the sky,
As we go, this we know,
God is nigh.[14]

And at Mecot's funeral, as with tradition, all that could be heard on that mountaintop was the bugler playing "Taps." The birds had stopped chirping. The wind had stopped its gentle breezes. The people had stopped whispering. And our crying had halted for that moment in time.

And I thought to myself: They are all here because Mecot, my American brother, has touched their lives in one way or another. And each one of them helped mold him into the proud Marine that he became.

---

[14] Jari Villanueva, *Twenty-Four Notes That Tap Deep Emotions: The Story of America's Most Famous Bugle Call*, (Baltimore: JV Music, 2001).

So how does a little boy born into a small American town become an
elite warrior for our country? Many young men and women daily make
this decision. It is a thoughtful, ultimate decision to risk one's life in order to defend our freedom. These special young men and women are
American heroes just like my American brother.

One definition of the word hero is "an illustrious warrior."[15] A hero is
someone who stands for strength, bravery, endurance, and humbleness.
We watch movies to see action heroes fight for a good cause, but we often ignore the real-life heroes whom we confront every day just like my
American brother.

Mecot was my hero, my American brother. An American brother just
like so many that are raised in small all-American towns with that one
common element: an innate desire to willingly serve and protect our
country and our freedom.

---

[15] Random House *Webster's College Dictionary*, 2nd ed., s.v. "hero."

22

Presentation of Awards

Real men, I believe, are sensitive, feeling people who freely express what they feel without fear of anyone regarding them as a pussy. It is the weak man who is always the one showing hardness, and no feeling. The weak man must prove himself strong. A real man has nothing to prove, and does not care what anyone thinks of his demeanor.

— Charles Henderson, CWO (Ret.), USMC.
Modern-day American author and journalist

THIS QUOTE WAS USED TO BEGIN A TRIBUTE TO Captain Mike Haskell by Charles Henderson. Henderson goes on to say: "My friend, Marine Captian "Iron Mike" Haskell, was a real man. He kissed his kids. He hugged his fellow Marines. He wept, sitting on an ammunition box one evening in Beirut, because he missed his wife, back home in Virginia."[16]

Mike Haskell served at the Barracks, 8th and I, in Washington, D.C., from 1978 to 1981, first as a second lieutenant, then as a first lieutenant, and finally, as a captain. He served as Charlie Company Commander, Weapons Company Commander, and as Fire and Air Support Coordinator with H&S Company.

Chief Warrant Officer GM Matthews wrote the following about Haskell:

---

[16] http://marines.togetherweserved.com/usmc/servlet/tws.webapp.WebApp?cmd=ShadowBox
Profile&type=Person&ID=41756

Mike Haskell was my Wpns Plt Commander in 1977 while assigned to I/3/9. He was one of several new 2dLt's reporting to 9thMar in early part of 1977. He was unique; prior enlisted, Vietnam Vet, Drill Instructor. He was hard, but would back you up if you were right, he would take care of you, and he would brawl with the best of us! In all, he was an outstanding Marine and Officer, my Mentor, and good friend. I hope that I can gather all the history on this outstanding Marine that will serve the memory of him justice. Mike Haskell was my Weapons Platoon Commander in 1977 while assigned to I/3/9. He was one of several new 2dLt's reporting to 9thMar in early part of 1977. He was unique; prior enlisted, Vietnam Vet, Drill Instructor. He was hard, but would back you up if you were right, he would take care of you, and he would brawl with the best of us! In all, he was an outstanding Marine and Officer, my Mentor, and good friend. I hope that I can gather all the history on this outstanding Marine that will serve the memory of him justice.[17]

Captain Michael S. "Iron Mike" Haskell was well respected among his fellow Marines, especially Mecot. Mecot spoke of him often and really looked up to him. He was a former enlisted infantryman like Mecot and was a drill instructor, a Vietnam veteran turned infantry officer. Much of the time, officers that were previously enlisted are referred to as "mustangs." They have a lot of respect from enlisted Marines because they know how it feels to do all the work and be in the trenches. It was Captain Haskell who wrote my brother's FITREP (fitness report).

The FITREP is how Marines are graded annually and semiannually. All of these reports measure a Marine's strengths and weaknesses and set the pace for achieving success in their career in the Marine Corps. According to Captain Haskell's report, my brother had EXCEPTIONAL

[17] Ibid.

proficiency and conduct marks. The highest you can achieve is 5.0, and he received some 5.0 marks along with 4.8 and 4.9s. That is pretty rare to achieve, especially in a grunt infantry unit. Those marks demonstrate how driven and dedicated Mecot was in his role as a Marine. The following is what Captain Haskell wrote in Mecot's fitness report.

> Sgt. Camara is a superb young NCO whose work has been outstanding. Currently holding a Staff Sergeant's position and leading a section of 17 Marines and one sailor. Sgt. Camara's performance has surpassed all expectations of what is normally associated with a Marine of his experience. Sgt. Camara's contributions to the company shipboard training program were immense and the dividends of his initiative, leadership, and ability to instruct have been witnessed. Sgt. Camara's section has been an integral part of Co. C's performance at two of its most vital, visible, and tactically significant areas. Of particular note were Sgt. Camara's performance and demonstrated courage, presence of mind, tactical proficiency, and leadership during several occasions when his section's positions were subjected to intense direct and indirect fire. During this arduous, demanding, challenging environment for any leader, Sgt. Camara's section has largely risen due to Sgt. Camara's leadership, maintained and even increased the camaraderie, morale, and togetherness that they have been known for throughout this deployment. This NCO's professional knowledge particularly in the technical and tactical aspects of the Dragon Weapon System is of level rarely attained by Marines of his grade. For his superior performance during this deployment Sgt. Camara has been recommended for a Navy Achievement Medal. I consider this NCO's growth potential to be virtually unlimited and would actively seek his services in any assignment.[18]

---

[18] USMC fitness report for Sgt. Mecot E. Camara, signed by Capt. Michael S. Haskell, September 30, 1983.

This report was signed by Captain Haskell on September 30, 1983. Captain Haskell did not survive the bombing.

Lieutenant Colonel Howard Gerlach, who had known Mecot, also remarked on Mecot's fitness report: "Sgt. Camara is a strong, personable Marine NCO who is accurately described by his company commander. He would be an asset to any unit which assigned. In my opinion he would be particularly effective as a Drill Instructor."[19] His remarks were dated October 11, 1983. Twelve days before Mecot was killed.

Mecot's love of the Marine Corps was known to his superiors. Prior to enlistment young men are molded by their families, community, and church. Once enlisted and part of the Marine Corps, they morph into true American brothers, during which hard work and respect for oneself, one's fellow Marines, and one's country are what drive them to succeed.

I know in my brother's case, all of those elements were the driving force that kept him moving up the chain of command. Mecot picked up sergeant in three years, which in the infantry is not an easy accomplishment. I believe, after many late-night discussions with his fellow Marines, that if he had lived he probably would have gone on to be a sergeant major—the highest rank you can achieve as an enlisted Marine.

I think some would have tried to peg Mecot as overambitious. Not me. He truly loved what he did and, as a result, he was great at it. And all his achievements never made him lose sight of Daddy's words of wisdom. Humbleness is the foundation of all virtues. My brother could not have been more humble: a true characteristic of an American brother. He was a significant success story for the brief time he served, and never did one hear him brag about his accomplishments.

Listed below are the rest of his awards:

---

[19] Addendum to the USMC fitness report for Sergeant Mecot E. Camara, signed by Lt. Col. Howard Gerlach, October 11, 1983.

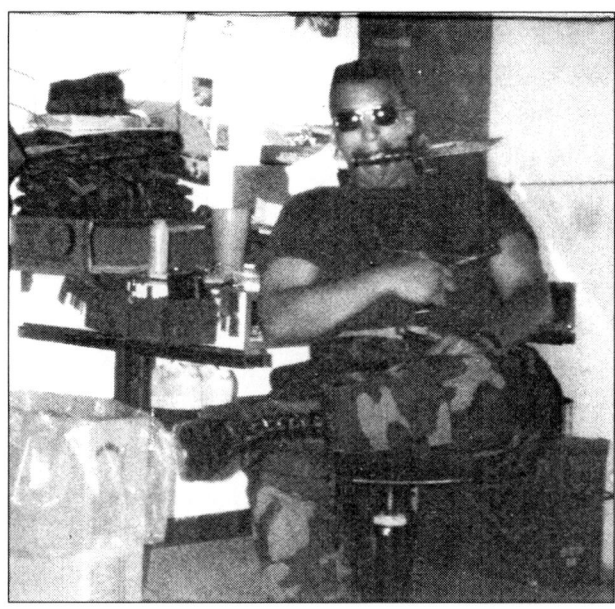

Mecot in his office in the BLT Headquarters Building in Beirut. This is the last photo of him before the bombing.

Meritorious Mast—Mecot received a Meritorious Mast as a lance corporal on February 3, 1983. It is not a medal or ribbon, but it is the second-highest letter you can receive in the Marine Corps. It was signed by his commanding officer, Lt. Col. Gerlach, who was at the Beirut bombing and survived the blast. And although it is not high up on the awards chart, it is very good to be able to get at a young rank such as lance corporal.

For Mecot's Meritorious Mast recognition, Lt. Col. Gerlach wrote,

For superior performance of duty while servicing as 2nd Section Gunner, Dragon Platoon, Weapons Company, 1st Battalion, 8th Marines from 6 December 1982 to 28 January 1983. During this period your performance has been unparalleled within the platoon. Your constant, aggressive leadership coupled with your exceptional knowledge has significantly contributed to the training and good order and discipline of the platoon. As NCOIC of vehicle maintenance you always ensured and conducted the proper platoon vehicle maintenance. Your initiative, bearing, and willingness to seek responsibility are quickly becoming hallmarks of your career. Through your outstanding efforts, you reflected great credit upon yourself, this Battalion, and the United States Marine Corps.[20]

Purple Heart—Mecot received a Purple Heart on December 7, 1983:

For professional achievement in the superior performance of duties while assigned to Battalion Landing Team (BLT) 1/8, 24th marine amphibious unit (MAU), Marine Amphibious Ready Group (MARG) 2-83. And during the period from 21 May 1983 to 23 October 1983, BLT 1/8 as the ground combat element of the 24th MAU who served with distinction as the Landing Force Sixth Fleet (LF6F) 2-83. From 28 May 1983 to 23 October 1983, BLT 1/8 also served as the ground force of the U.S. Contingent of the Multi-National Force (MNF) in Beirut, Lebanon. Assigned to the most southern sector of responsibility of the MNF, BLT 1/8 established a perimeter around the Beirut International Airport and positions at the Lebanese University. In the accomplishment of its peace keeping mission, the BLT conducted approximately 1,032 foot patrols in its sector and 344 motorized patrols throughout Beirut.

---

[20] Lt. Col. Howard Gerlach, Meritorious Mast letter to LCpl. Mecot E. Camara, February 3, 1983.

The BLT also became heavily involved in the training of the Lebanese Armed Forces from basic entry level OCS leadership training. Courses of instruction covered such diverse subjects as patrolling, close combat, physical training, weapons, communications, helicopterborne operations, demolitions, first aid, SPIE rigging/repelling, and tank operations. In addition, the BLT provided basic instruction in fire direction center procedures, basic cannoneering and maintenance for the first initial LAF 198 Howitzer Battalion.

The BLT not only worked closely with the other members of the MNF operationally, but spent significant time in cross-training with our British, French, and Italian Allies. The tactics and techniques along with the friendships established solidified the Multi-National Force's resolve in its mission in Lebanon. Also of significant note is the special mission assigned to the BLT to supplement the security of both the U.S. Consulate and the British Embassy. The Marines assigned to this task were under constant threat and always alert for potential danger. Their role in allowing the diplomatic functions of the Embassies to continue under relatively normal conditions greatly enhanced the Department of State's ability to accomplish its mission.

On several occasions the BLT's combat readiness was tested as a result [of] overt hostile actions by factions opposed to the government [of] Lebanon. Employing both direct and indirect fire weapons systems, these actions were directed against both USMNF joint checkpoints and the BIA complex. In every instance the Marines and Sailors demonstrated their resolve and resilience. Through a coordinated team effort they responded to each challenge in a superb manner.

The discipline and professionalism that the Marines displayed left a lasting impression in the minds of the MNF personnel and the many visitors to Lebanon (to include the Secretary of State, Senators, and Representatives, Chairman of the Joint Chiefs of Staff, the Secretary of the Navy, the Commandant of the Marine Corps, and the Commander, U.S. Sixth Fleet) that observed them in their duties. Their superb performance substantiated the previous esteem in which the United States Marines has been held in the Mediterranean Sea area since their initial arrival in 1949.[21]

Combat Action Ribbon (CAR)—Mecot received the highly respected CAR for his service in Beirut as part of the Multi-National Peacekeeping Force. Marines can instantly see it and know that you were in combat.

Navy and Marine Corps Achievement Medal (NAM)—Mecot received the NAM posthumously in December 1984 for his stellar performance. As cited by Major General A. M. Gray, Mecot was awarded the NAM

> For professional achievement in the superior performance of his duties while serving as a member of Battalion Landing Team 1/8, 24th Marine Amphibious Unit, Fleet Marine Force, Atlantic from 21 May 1983 to 23 October 1983. During this period Sgt. Camara was deployed with his unit to Beirut, Lebanon, as a member of the Multi-National Peacekeeping Force, assigned peace keeping missions in and around the Beirut Airport Complex, the Lebanese University, and external security for the United States Consulate and the British Embassy. Additionally, extensive training was con-

---

[21] Gen. P. X. Kelley, Purple Heart citation for Sgt. Mecot E. Camara, December 7, 1983.

ducted with the Lebanese Armed Forces and the other members of the Multi-National Peacekeeping Force. Sgt. Camara's support and assistance in the important task was noteworthy.

The tactics and techniques learned along with the friendships he established helped solidify the Multi-National Forces' resolve in its mission. On the numerous occasions when combat readiness and resolve were tested, Sgt. Camara's presence of mind under fire and outstanding performance of duty resulted in a coordinated team effort which demonstrated the dedication and resilience of the Battalion Landing Team Marines and Sailors. The discipline and professionalism that he displayed left a lasting impression on the leaders of the Multi-National Forces and the many dignitaries who visited this war-torn area and directly contributed to the Government of Lebanon's efforts to restore peace and stability to the country. Sgt. Camara's professionalism and loyal devotion to duty, reflected great credit upon himself, the Marine Corps, and the United States Naval Service.[22]

Navy Unit Commendation (NUC)—Mecot and his unit received the NUC on January 21, 1984. Hs Mediterranean Amphibious Ready Group performed extraordinarily well in combat and noncombat missions.

Good Conduct Medal—Mecot received the Good Conduct Medal on November 1, 1983, for not getting in trouble (or at least not getting caught—he has always had that mischievous side of him that he never outgrew) for a three-year period. It was issued by E. W. Cassidy, head of the Decorations and Medals Branch, by direction of the commandant of the Marine Corps. Issued with the medal was this statement from Cassidy:

---

[22] Maj. Gen. A. M. Gray, Navy and Marine Corps Achievement Medal citation for Sgt. Mecot E. Camara, December 1984.

Given to Sgt. Mecot E. Camara, U.S. Marine Corps, having conducted yourself in a creditable manner, you are, by direction of the Commandant of the Marine Corps, awarded a Good Conduct Medal First Award for the period 7 January 1981 to 23 October 1983. Your conduct during this period denotes honest and faithfulness in keeping with the highest traditions of the Marine Corps.

Marine Corps Expeditionary Medal—Mecot and his entire unit received the Marine Corps Expeditionary Medal for making special deployment.

Sea Service Deployment Ribbon (SSDR)—Mecot received the SSDR for deployment on a ship for over thirty consecutive days.

Mecot's awards demonstrate that he was destined to become a great asset to the Marines. His passion to make a difference and serve selflessly continued until his last breath. He lived, bled, and died a true American brother. As stated by General P. X. Kelley, commandant of U.S. Marine Corps,

> Mecot's service in the Marine Corps demonstrated his special personal commitment to our nation and its security. Although I realize there is little that can be said which will lesson your grief, I want you to know how much all Marines personally appreciate his commitment and sacrifice. Along with a grateful nation, we are proud of Mecot. My prayers and the payers of the Marines who served with him are with you and your family.[23]

---

[23] Gen. P. X. Kelley, letter to Mrs. B. J. Camara, the author's mother, December 9, 1983.

Back to College via Parris Island

AFTER BURYING MY HIGHLY ACCOMPLISHED U.S. Marine brother, and after the memorial services in North Carolina, I stayed at home for a few more days. I wanted to make sure Mom and Tammy were going to be OK. Tammy decided to live in the downstairs of our home with Echo. She wanted some time to think about her future in a familiar place that held so many good memories for her and Mecot. Additionally, she was surrounded by most of our family since we lived upstairs and my sister and her family lived down the hillside. And she was minutes away from her family too.

She had lots of memories in the basement rooms with Mecot. They were our game rooms growing up, complete with a poker table, ping-pong, a huge toy room, a huge laundry room, and a large kitchen and bar. Daddy had added a bedroom and bathroom for overnight guests. It was where they spent their honeymoon night.

It was perfect for Tammy and Echo. I think it was comforting for her to be where Mecot and she had shared so much life together.

Sometimes late at night, I would hear her crying. I would always go downstairs to check on her. She would be holding his picture and the most recent letter from him. She was still receiving letters after he died. That was very devastating. Sometimes we would talk about the notion that maybe he was still alive and living in Beirut and the letters would keep coming until we found him. But the reality of this historic event always crept back into our minds. He was gone forever.

She would try to hide her face in a towel so as not to wake Echo with her wailing. She did not want anyone, including me, to see her so distraught. She was trying to be strong for Echo and everyone else.

However, when she would remove the towel to breathe, her face was beet-red, with tears streaming down her cheeks. Her nose was dripping down to her upper lip, which could not stop quivering. I would just sit with her and hold her hand. There were no words that came to my mind. I just wanted her to know I was with her. And I shared her pain. Eventually her tears would stop. It would come in waves. Some days were good days and some days were hard days. Eventually, the letters stopped coming.

So coming back home to Hinton was the best thing for Tammy. She and Mecot had lots of their friends back home. They came to visit her often. And her family was just down the road, and they stayed with her and Echo as much as they could.

Often Mecot's best friend in the Marines, named Butch, would come to visit. He came all the way from Pensacola, Florida. He used to hang out with them at Camp Lejuene all the time. She was very fond of Butch, knowing him as "Mecot's best friend in the Corps."

Tammy shared her story of their connection as follows:

> Butch called me in December [1983] after returning to base from float. He was wondering how we all were and, of course, we had tons of questions about Mecot for him. He offered to come and visit us so we could ask the questions we wanted. His first visit to the Camara house, where we were living in the basement, was in January of 1984. Echo fell in love with him. Butch bought him a puppet and a truck. Butch was very funny too, and Echo just loved him. Butch made plans to come back to see us a month later. Then on his third trip to see us I decided to

move back to North Carolina. We began to have feelings for each other shortly thereafter. The most important thing to me was that Echo loved him. My love for him came a little bit later, though. Butch didn't actually propose to me. We both decided to get married May 15, 1984. We moved to Richmond, Virginia, for work after Butch got out of the Marine Corps. Then we moved back to Hinton when Echo was three years old. Echo did attend Bellepoint Elementary School there.

They bought a home in Hinton and lived there for a short while. Echo started his elementary years exactly where his father started—at Bellepoint Elementary.

Many a day you could catch Tammy sitting in Rover (she kept the jeep) at the school. She parked facing the direction of the playground. Every afternoon for months she would sit in Rover and watch Echo play at recess.

A few years passed and she had two more children with Butch—a daughter name Leia and a son named Preston.

Moreover, it was a life adjustment for all of us not having Mecot with us anymore. Tammy survived with the great support and love of Butch.

Although she was heartbroken and devastated, she worked through the pain. It was comforting knowing she married Mecot's best friend and someone who knew exactly the hurt and devastation she was feeling. Butch did as Mecot wished and vowed to take care of Rat.

Our mom survived; however, she would never be the same. Losing her husband and her only son fewer than two years apart greatly impacted her outlook on life. She definitely had hard days, but she was a strong-willed woman. She somehow managed to keep moving forward every day with a smile on her face determined to make peace with the adversity and emptiness in her heart. It was comforting to me knowing that my older sister was just down the mountainside from her. Mom focused her time on Echo, and on my sister's children. Her new role as nanny really kept her busy and happy. She always had a big tub of blocks and toys for the grandkids at our home.

I knew the time was nearing for me to return to college. A few weeks after the funeral, Mom insisted that I go back to Queens College to resume my freshman year. I was scared to go back because I had missed so much school work and I was significantly behind. I felt failure was a definite possibility but I had to at least try. Mecot taught me to never give up.

The day had come. It was so hard leaving home and driving back by myself. I felt as if someone had taken a knife and cut a huge piece of my heart out and left it buried with my brother. I hugged Mom, Tammy, li'l Echo, my sister and Ronnie, and their children good-bye.

I did not want to leave but I knew I had to at least try my best to get back on track at college. Mecot was whispering in my ear from heaven, "Get your ass back to college and make something of yourself for me." I slowly backed down our long driveway in tears.

I kept driving along Greenbrier Drive sobbing and thinking about Mecot. My mind was spinning with childhood memories and the devastation of the bombing, still trying to understand how he died, what he died for, and whether he was he really not coming back and maybe they had made a mistake.

I could not get myself together. I needed a moment to think. I had an early start that morning and going back to Queens was not what I wanted to do. I decided to take a little detour out of the way. That detour turned into a not-so-little road trip.

I pulled over at the Bluestone Lake Overlook and mapped out the way to Parris Island, South Carolina. It would take eight hours. I pulled out my AAA flip map that I always kept in my car. Daddy always had us keep an AAA map of the United States in each car just in case we could not find our way home.

So off I went. I took off the T-tops on my Buick Regal and sang at the top of my lungs. It was too pretty of a day and I figured the fresh mountain air would feel great on my skin and even better passing through my lungs. I needed to just breathe and sing. Singing made me happy and reminded me of many a road trip I took in Rover with Mecot.

This road trip was before cell phones, GPS, and Pandora. It was me and my AAA flip map and good ole' radio stations to keep me going. Lots of songs were playing that reminded me of Mecot. Of course there was "Freebird" by Lynyrd Skynrd (one of his all-time favorites) and songs by Hank Williams, Jr., Blondie, Bachman-Turner Overdrive, and Supertramp. I sang all the way to Parris Island. I must have heard all his favorite tunes a dozen times each.

I just wanted all my senses to take in what he took in on that day in January as he rode the bus there. I knew I would never be back to Parris Island ever again, so I thought it would only be appropriate to have one more final moment where Mecot started his U.S. Marine career.

I justified this lengthy road trip as a way to complete my closure of his death. Although later in life, I realized there is never any closure when you lose your brother, especially your only brother.

So I made it to Parris Island. I drove to the front gate and stopped to ask permission to drive on the base. The sentry guards had never been approached by a young, seventeen-year-old female just wanting to cruise around on base. This was probably a first. But so were the circumstances. I explained, while trying to be tough and hold back tears, that my brother was one of the Marines killed in the Beirut bombing and I wanted to visit here one last time to see where my brother began his military career. The guards respectfully asked me to wait while they made a call. I am not sure who they called, but permission was granted for me to gain entrance into the base for the afternoon. One of the guards handed me a base pass and I slowly drove forward.

I really did not know the base well at all. I had only been there once, and that was for Mecot's spectacular graduation ceremony; however, I did witness a platoon of new recruits getting off the bus and walking through those infamous doors that read, THROUGH THESE PORTALS PASS PROSPECTS FOR THE WORLD'S FINEST FIGHTING FORCE: UNITED STATES MARINES.

That's really all I needed to witness. I felt a sense of admiration and empathy simultaneously. I did not have the only American brother. There are many that walk through that portal every day of their own free will and for the good of our country.

And those young men and women were going to go through the toughest training of their lives. Pain, sweat, tears that all lead to becoming a tough, driven warrior. This was the empathy that I felt when recalling Mecot's letters that he wrote me while there.

While I drove around base, it came full circle to me and I realized that for an American brother, like Mecot, a strong reason for many to join the Marine Corps was for a sense of belonging.

Many young men and women want to feel a sense of commitment and loyalty that connects them to future groups they may join later in life.

The brotherhood found in the Marine Corps is legendary; Marines put the Marine to the left and right ahead of themselves. This spirit of *semper fidelis*—always faithful—is something they can't find anywhere else.

For it is here that ambitious, smart, and motivated young men and women who want to be part of a prestigious organization are drawn as America's most elite fighting force. I saw them. And they, just like Mecot, have exactly what it takes to become an American brother.

As I drove off the base, I witnessed a new platoon of recruits marching in succession, carrying heavily weighted backpacks loaded with gear.

It explained to me that, perhaps, my brother was one of many all-American small-town heroes that choose to become American patriots. Each one comes with an amazing life story too.

I could hear them chanting the same cadence that Mecot once taught me: "Birdie, birdie in the sky. Drop a little whitewash in my eye. I'm no sailor, I won't cry. I'm just glad that cows don't fly."

That cadence so made me smile. And it warmed my cold, saddened heart. I felt as if Mecot was riding right next to me with that smirky grin, shouting that cadence right along with them. As the sun was setting through my rearview mirror, I started my car, put it in drive, popped in Mecot's favorite Lynyrd Skynyrd cassette, pushed play, and drove off wearing a peaceful smile when I heard this line from "Freebird": If I leave here tomorrow / Would you still remember me?

Mecot graduated from Parris Island April of 1981. His footprints will forever be imprinted in this soil as far as I am concerned. A piece of him rests here for this is where his time came to be an American brother.

I still remember him and I will never forget him. As a nation, we must never forget those we know who have served or are currently serving in the United States military. We must never forget the historical tragedy of October 23, 1983, for the U.S. Marine Corps. And, more importantly, we must never forget that life does march on.

Epilogue

Life's Forward March and Lessons Learned

TAMMY AND BUTCH ARE STILL MARRIED and living in West Virginia. He is a coal miner and she is a nurse. They are the blessed grandparents to Kahlan Camara. She is Mecot's only grandchild, born to Mecot Jr. and Andrea Camara, who also live in West Virginia.

Our mother passed away in 2009. My sister and I currently live in Florida. Over the years, we have shared many larger-than-life tales of Uncle Mecot to our own children, who now range in age from twelve to thirty-one years.

Our children will never know my American brother. He was taken much too soon from us. But the stories that are told about him are legendary in the Camara family and throughout all of Hinton.

Most especially, my oldest son, Joe, knows the importance of his Uncle Mecot's call to duty on a personal level. Joe's experience was the driving force for me to write this book in honor of my American brother and all those serving in our military.

Joe was attending his first session at Florida State University in the summer of 2011. I figured his starting in summer was a great way for him to get acclimated to college life, get familiar with this large campus, and get used to not living at home.

By way of Facebook and a few calls from my "mommy friends" who also have sons in Tallahassee, I was immediately notified that it appeared Joe had been in a fight. Joe had never been in a fight in his entire life! Yes, I saw the pictures and he looked a little roughed up. Not bad. A really large scrape on his leg was about the most damage to his sturdy body that I noticed. He hadn't gained the freshman fifteen yet and his lacrosse training from high school helped him maintain his sturdy physique.

I called to check on him. Joe adamantly replied to me, "I am fine. I am absolutely fine. I do not want to talk about it." While he was yelling this in my ear, I saw on Facebook that an adorable young lady had taken care of his wounds on his leg. I called three times a day for the next few days just to make sure he was OK. I got the standard answer: "I am fine. I am absolutely fine. I do not want to talk about it."

It was never discussed again until he came home. And one day while I took him shopping at the local mall, we sat down together to have lunch in the food court. Joe ordered his favorite: Chick-fil-A sandwich, fries, and a Sprite. I, on the other hand, ordered a big juicy burger and Coca-Cola from Burger King.

It was a delightful lunch, just the two of us. It is a rarity when you are the mother of three sons to get that one-on-one time together, and it is such a big treat! My other two sons were off hitting lacrosse balls together, and I was thrilled to be having lunch with Joe. He had been away attending summer session for the past month and I was so glad to have him home if only for a few weeks.

Of all things, at lunch, Joe decided to bring up his infamous FSU fight. "Mom, I never told you what happened, and I think I should let you know now so here it goes." He started the explanation with a question: "Mom, what would you do if someone was making fun of Uncle Mecot?" I had just taken my first bite of my super juicy burger, and my jaw dropped wide open and my first bite fell right out of my mouth. I replied, "What?"

"You heard me. What would you do if someone was making fun of Uncle Mecot?"

"Well…" I slowly shook my head and more burger fell out of my mouth. And before I could give him an answer he started talking.

Joe tells the story like this:

> I was having a great time meeting lots of hot chicks and just hangin' out, when this scrawny guy approached me and made fun of my red, white, and blue shorts that I was wearing in honor of the Fourth of July. He said they were stupid. I was raised by my mom to always walk away from ignorant people that say mean things. So I did just that and walked away from this smart ass and continued to have a fun night.
>
> Off to the next party. I was getting a good feel for college life and I was loving it! My friends and our new hot chick friends proceeded to the next party. It was getting close to the fireworks going off and everyone was in a super festive mood. We were all gathered on the deck of one of the frat houses, ready to watch, when what to my wondering eyes should appear. Smart Ass again.
>
> And again, he said my shorts were stupid. He said, "Dude, you haven't taken those things off yet? You look like a fool wearing red, white, and blue shorts for the Fourth of July. Why'd you even buy them? They're dumb."
>
> Once again, I made the good choice and walked away. I was raised with you telling me at least three times a day to always make good choices.
>
> I'd about had enough of him. Thank goodness the fun I was having totally outweighed the frustration brought on by stupid remarks coming from a now slightly intoxicated, belligerent smart ass.
>
> The night progressed nicely. Fireworks were going off in bright reds and blues over the capitol while patriotic songs were being played in simulcast. And everyone was singing

with the music. I knew I was going to love my college experience at FSU.

So, once the spectacular show of booming blues and reds was finished, we all decided to go to McDonald's for some late-night grub. We thought we were the only ones to come up with that idea. I was wrong. The line to order was getting longer and longer.

As I looked back to see how long the line was getting behind me, who do I make eye contact with? It's Smart Ass again. And here he comes, staggering up to my face, "I can't believe you are still wearing those stupid shorts." I ignored him. By this time we had gotten our grub to go and we were all walking back to the dorm. And who do I hear walking behind us? He then yells down the sidewalk of our dorm, "So, what's it to you anyway?"

In my mind I had had enough. I dropped my tasty McDonald's grub and I screamed back. "I'll tell you what it means to me: My uncle bled these colors as a U.S. Marine. He was a sergeant that died so idiots like you are free to live in this great country and free to shout rude, unpatriotic comments like idiots!" Mom, I took him down to the ground and beat his ass.

I looked at Joe with tears in my eyes and softly said, "You know, I have raised you with the belief that fighting is wrong. No matter what, you do not fight; you walk away and never hit anyone."

Joe, with his head held low, replied, "Yes, Mom."

And then I spoke even softer and asked him, "But did you get 'em good?"

Joe raised his head, grinned a smirky grin, and responded, "I sure did."

Acknowledgments

T hank you to the following individuals without whose contributions and support this book would not have been written:

Kay Dorenbos, author and editor whose creative mind and sound advice began my journey to complete this book.

Staff Sergeant Levi J. Deniston, USMC, whose loyalty and love for his fallen brothers prevails, as demonstrated in his willingness to always and unselfishly give of his time to assist me with every military segment of my brother's story.

Harley Patrick, Hellgate Press, whose willingness to consider my brother's story relevant and worthy of being published.

Michael Trudeau, professional editor, whose patience and understanding of what I wanted to say evolved into the words and meaning of *American Brother.*

Charles Henderson, well-known and respected author and retired U.S. Marine, who, without hesitation, so kindly agreed to share his memories of my brother in the Foreword.

Ryan Thompson, whose time, effort and design lead to the beginnings of the *American Brother* website.

Douglas and Elizabeth Nelson of NelsonCreative, whose neighborly act of love and professional services created the beautiful book cover.

Captain Chuck Valence, USMC (Retired); 1st Sgt Douglas Hester, USMC; Commander Mike Gentz, Island X-4 Seabees; Maxwell Preddy (cover model) whose team efforts lead to the successful completion of the book cover (i.e., Mecot's dress blues uniform recreated to nearly exact rank and specification).

Lastly, my best friends forever, Angela Bellows, Dianne Santana, Sharon Mays, Vicky Preddy, Carol King, Janet Powell, Carol Young,

Kamber Cooper, Rachel Handwerk, Nancy Richmond and Richie Cantrell, Jen and Steve Shevenell (USMC, retired), Denese and Joseph R. Dean (U.S. Army, retired) and my sweet family. Thank you for your love.

Appendix

M ECOT'S FELLOW AMERICAN BROTHERS WHO DIED with him that fateful date in history, October 23, 1983, as well as those who died pre-bombing while serving on this peacekeeping mission from 1982 to 1983, are listed below. Also included are the post-bombing victims who later died from injuries sustained in the attack, and four others who have died since. Two of these died in nonhostile incidents, and two died on September 11, 2001, in the attack on the Twin Towers.

Grateful acknowledgment to Staff Sergeant Levi Deniston, United States Marine Corps, for the accuracy of this list.

PRE-BOMBING

Cpl David L. Reagan—KIA on 30 September 1982
Cpl Robert V. McMaugh—KIA on 18 April 1983 (embassy bombing)
1st Lt Donald G. Losely Jr.—KIA on 29 April 1983
SSgt Alexander M. Ortega—KIA on 29 April 1983
Cpl Pedro J. Valle—KIA on 6 September 1983
LCpl Randy W. Clark—KIA on 6 September 1983
SSgt Alan H. Soifert—KIA on 14 October 1983
Capt Michael J. Ohler—KIA on 16 October 1983

BOMBING 23 October 1983

Unites States Marine Corps
Maj Andrew L. Davis
Maj Paul A. Hein
Maj John W. Macroglou
Maj William E. Winter

Capt Joseph J. Boccia Jr.

Capt Michael S. Haskell

Capt Peter J. Scialabba

Capt Vincent L. Smith

Capt Walter E. Wint Jr.

1st Lt John N. Boyette

1st Lt Maurice E. Hukill

1st Lt David J. Nairn

1st Lt Clyde W. Plymel

1st Lt Charles J. Schnorf

1st Lt William S. Sommerhof

1st Lt Donald E. Woollett

1st Lt William A. Zimmerman

CWO3 Richard C. Ortiz

WO Paul G. Innocenzi III

SgtMaj Frederick B. Douglass

1st Sgt David L. Battle

1st Sgt Tandy W. Wells

MSgt Roy L. Edwards

MSgt Matilde J. Hernandez Jr.

MSgt Richard L. Lemnah

MSgt John L. Pearson

MSgt Scipio Williams Jr.

GySgt Donald W. Hildreth

GySgt Edward E. Kimm

GySgt Charlie R. Martin

GySgt Charles R. Ray

GySgt Lloyd D. West

SSgt John R. Bohnet Jr.

SSgt Kevin P. Coulman

SSgt Leland E. Gann

SSgt Ronald J. Garcia

SSgt Harold D. Ghumm

SSgt Richard J. Holberton

SSgt William H. Pollard

SSgt Patrick K. Prindeville

SSgt Thomas G. Smith

SSgt Thomas P. Thorstad

SSgt John R. Weyl

Sgt Richard D. Blankenship

Sgt Leon Bohannon Jr.

Sgt John J. Bonk Jr.

Sgt Anthony K. Brown

Sgt Mecot E. Camara

Sgt Robert A. Conley

Sgt Charles D. Cook

Sgt Rick R. Crudale

Sgt Steven M. Forrester

Sgt Timothy R. Giblin

Sgt Robert E. Greaser

Sgt Freddie Haltiwanger Jr.

Sgt Gilbert Hanton

Sgt Thomas C. Keown

Sgt Michael S. LaRiviere

Sgt Steven B. LaRiviere

Sgt Val S. Lewis

Sgt Michael R. Massman

Sgt James E. McDonough

Sgt Richard M. Menkins II

Sgt Michael D. Mercer

Sgt Harry D. Myers

Sgt John A. Olsen

Sgt Joseph A. Owens

Sgt John A. Phillips Jr.

Sgt Rafael I. Pomales-Torres
Sgt Juan C. Rodriquez
Sgt Ronald L. Shallo
Sgt Allen D. Wesley
Sgt Burton Wherland Jr.
Sgt Jeffrey D. Young
Cpl Terry W. Abbott
Cpl Moses J. Arnold Jr.
Cpl Nicholas Baker
Cpl Richard E. Barrett
Cpl David R. Bousum
Cpl Bobby S. Buchanon Jr.
Cpl John B. Buckmaster
Cpl Paul A. Callahan
Cpl Bert D. Corcoran
Cpl Brett A. Croft
Cpl Timothy J. Dunnigan
Cpl Michael D. Fulcher
Cpl Michael S. Fulton
Cpl William R. Gaines Jr.
Cpl Sean R. Gallagher
Cpl David D. Gay
Cpl Davin M. Green
Cpl Ferrandy D. Henderson
Cpl Stanley G. Hester
Cpl Bruce L. Howard
Cpl Edward F. Iacovino Jr.
Cpl James J. Jackowski
Cpl Edward A. Johnston
Cpl Steven Jones
Cpl James C. Knipple
Cpl Thomas G. Lamb

Cpl David A. Lewis

Cpl Joseph R. Livingston Jr.

Cpl Paul D. Lyon Jr.

Cpl Samuel Maitland Jr.

Cpl David S. Massa

Cpl Timothy D. McNeely

Cpl Joseph P. Moore Sgt

Cpl John F. Muffler

Cpl Alejandro Munoz

Cpl Connie Ray Page

Cpl Thomas S. Perron

Cpl Victor M. Prevatt

Cpl Warren Richardson

Cpl Louis J. Rotondo

Cpl Michael C. Sauls

Cpl Gary R. Scott

Cpl Thomas A. Shipp

Cpl James F. Silvia

Cpl Kirk H. Smith

Cpl Edward Soares Jr.

Cpl Stephen E. Spencer

Cpl Jeffrey G. Stokes

Cpl Thomas D. Stowe

Cpl Devon L. Sundar

Cpl Dennis A. Thompson

Cpl Eric R. Walker

Cpl Leonard W. Walker

Cpl Eric G. Washington

Cpl Obrian Weekes

Cpl Johnny A. Williamson

Cpl John E. Wolfe

Cpl Craig L. Wyche

LCpl Clemon S. Alexander
LCpl John R. Allman
LCpl Johansen Banks
LCpl James R. Baynard
LCpl Stephen B. Bland
LCpl John W. Blocker
LCpl Jeffrey L. Boulos
LCpl David W. Brown
LCpl Bradley J. Campus
LCpl Johnnie D. Ceasar
LCpl Curtis J. Cooper
LCpl Johnny L. Copeland
LCpl David L. Cosner
LCpl Kevin P. Custard
LCpl Russell E. Cyzick
LCpl Michael J. Devlin
LCpl Thomas B. DiBenedetto
LCpl Jesse J. Ellison
LCpl Danny R. Estes
LCpl Sean F. Estler
LCpl Benjamin E. Fuller
LCpl David B. Gander
LCpl George M. Gangur
LCpl Randall J. Garcia
LCpl Warner Gibbs Jr.
LCpl Richard J. Gordon
LCpl Harold F. Gratton
LCpl Thomas A. Hairston
LCpl Virgil D. Hamilton
LCpl William Hart
LCpl Douglas E. Held
LCpl Mark A. Helms

LCpl Bruce A. Hollingshead
LCpl Lyndon J. Hugh
LCpl Jeffrey W. James
LCpl Thomas A. Julian
LCpl Walter V. Kingsly
LCpl Freas H. Kreischer III
LCpl Keith J. Laise
LCpl James J. Langon IV
LCpl Joseph J. Mattacchione
LCpl Timothy R. McMahon
LCpl Louis Melendez-Cruz
LCpl Ronald W. Meurer
LCpl Richard A. Morrow
LCpl Luis A. Nava
LCpl Ulysses G. Parker
LCpl Mark W. Payne
LCpl James C. Price
LCpl David M. Randolph
LCpl Guillermo San Pedro Jr.
LCpl Gerald D. Shropshire
LCpl Stanley J. Sliwinski
LCpl Michael C. Spaulding
LCpl John W. Spearing
LCpl Bill J. Stelpflug
LCpl Horace R. Stephens Jr.
LCpl Craig S. Stockton
LCpl Eric D. Sturghill
LCpl John J. Tishmack
LCpl Lex D. Trahan
LCpl Donald H. Vallone Jr.
LCpl Stephen B. Wentworth
LCpl Dwayne W. Wigglesworth

LCpl Rodney J. Williams
PFC Charles K. Bailey
PFC William F. Burley
PFC Marc L. Cole
PFC Juan M. Comas
PFC Sidney J. Decker
PFC Nathaniel G. Dorsey
PFC Richard A. Fluegel
PFC Michael A. Hastings
PFC Melvin D. Holmes
PFC John J. Ingalls
PFC Jack L. Martin
PFC Robert P. Olson
PFC Jeffrey B. Owen
PFC Eric A. Pulliam
PFC Rui A. Relvas
PFC Terrence L. Rich
PFC Scott L. Schultz
PFC Stephen D. Tingley

United States Navy
LtJG John R. Hudson
SA Scott E. Barnes
CHM George W. Peircy
HM1 Ronny K. Bates
HM2 Robert S. Holland
HM2 Michael H. Johnson
HM2 Marion E. Kees
HM2 George N. McVicker II
HM3 William D. Elliott Jr.
HM3 James E. Faulk
HM3 William B. Foster Jr.

HM3 David E. Worley
HM3 Joseph P. Milano
HM3 Diomedes J. Quirante
HN Jesse W. Beamon
HN Jimmy R. Cain
HN Bryan L. Earle

United States Army
SP4 Marcus A. Coleman
Sgt Daniel S. Cluck
SFC James G. Yarber

POST-BOMBING

LCpl John McCall—Died on 24 October 1983*
GySgt Alvin B. Belmer—Died on 30 October 1983*
LCpl Nathaniel W. Jenkins—Died on 30 October 1983*
Cpl Henry J. Townsend—Died on 2 December 1983*
Sgt Manuel A. Cox—KIA on 4 December 1983
Cpl Shannon D. Biddle—KIA on 4 December 1983
Cpl Sam Cherman—KIA on 4 December 1983
Cpl David L. Daugherty—KIA on 4 December 1983
Cpl Thomas A. Evans—KIA on 4 December 1983
Cpl Todd A. Kraft—KIA on 4 December 1983
Cpl Marvin H. Perkins—KIA on 4 December 1983
LCpl Jeffrey T. Hattaway—KIA on 4 December 1983
Cpl Terry L. Hudsen—Died on 5 December 1983*
Sgt Edward J. Gargano—KIA on 8 January 1984
LCpl George L. Dramis—KIA on 30 January 1984
LCpl Rodolfo Hernandez—Died on 8 February 1984 from combat
   injuries on 30 January 1984
Maj Alfred L. Butler III—Died on 9 February 1984
SSgt John W. Hendrickson—Died on 13 April 1990*

Col William R. Higgins—KIA on 6 July 1990

LCpl Larry H. Simpson Jr.—Died on 31 August 1992*

From wounds sustained on the barracks bombing on 23 October 1983.

OTHERS

GySgt James Paige Jr., USMC—Died on 9 December 1999 (nonhostile, active-duty helicopter training accident)

SSgt Scott N. Germosen—KIA on 9 January 2002 (nonhostile helicopter crash, OEF combat missions, Pakistan)

Firefighter John G. Chipura—KIA on 11 September 2001, Twin Towers

Firefighter Matthew D. Garvey 9 (retired GySgt)—KIA on 11 September 2001, Twin Towers

This book is written in honor, love, and respect to these service members and the survivors. My brother would have wanted it no other way.